Poems

by

Sir John Salusbury and
Robert Chester.

Early English Text Society.
Extra Series, No. CXIII.
1914 (*for* 1913).
Price 15*s*.

OXFORD: HORACE HART
PRINTER TO THE UNIVERSITY

Poems
by
Sir John Salusbury and Robert Chester.

WITH AN INTRODUCTION BY

CARLETON BROWN.

LONDON:
PUBLISHED FOR THE EARLY ENGLISH TEXT SOCIETY,
BY KEGAN PAUL, TRENCH, TRÜBNER & CO., Ltd.,
68–74 CARTER LANE, E.C.,
AND BY HUMPHREY MILFORD, OXFORD UNIVERSITY PRESS,
AMEN CORNER, E.C.

OXFORD
UNIVERSITY PRESS

Great Clarendon Street, Oxford OX2 6DP
United Kingdom

Oxford University Press is a department of the University of Oxford.
It furthers the University's objective of excellence in research, scholarship,
and education by publishing worldwide. Oxford is a registered trade mark of
Oxford University Press in the UK and in certain other countries

© The Early English Text Society 1914 (for 1913)

The moral rights of the authors have been asserted

Database right Oxford University Press (maker)

First Edition published in 1914 (for 1913)

All rights reserved. No part of this publication may be reproduced,
stored in a retrieval system, or transmitted, in any form or by any means,
without the prior permission in writing of Oxford University Press,
or as expressly permitted by law, or under terms agreed with the appropriate
reprographics rights organization. Enquiries concerning reproduction
outside the scope of the above should be sent to the Rights Department,
Oxford University Press, at the address above

You must not circulate this book in any other form
and you must impose this same condition on any acquirer

Published in the United States of America by Oxford University Press
198 Madison Avenue, New York, NY 10016, United States of America

British Library Cataloguing in Publication Data
Data available

Library of Congress Cataloging in Publication Data
Data available

Extra Series, 113

ISBN 978-0-85-991712-4

FOREWORDS

DURING the last two decades of the reign of Elizabeth poetry was in the very air, and obscure as well as great men caught the contagion of verse-making. It is with the verse of some of these obscure men that the present volume is concerned. If judged on their own merits these pieces might perhaps have been left in the oblivion in which they have remained for over three centuries. But though having in themselves no importance as literature, they throw additional light upon poems by Shakspere and other great Elizabethans : *alia claritas solis, alia claritas lunae.*

In presenting this material to the reader, I gladly take the opportunity of expressing my thanks to those who have in many ways courteously forwarded my investigation. To H. W. Blunt, Esq., M.A., Librarian of Christ Church, Oxford, I am indebted for according me liberal facilities for examining the Christ Church manuscript, and to the Archbishop Wake's Trustees for granting leave to print the poems contained in it. I have also to thank the Secretary to the Delegates of the Clarendon Press, C. Cannan, Esq., for the free use of rotographs of these poems. To S. R. Christie-Miller, Esq., of Britwell Court, I am under obligations for permission to reprint poems from the unique copy of the Parry volume, which is preserved in his library. I should add that it was a friendly suggestion supplied by A. W. Pollard, Esq., of the British Museum, which enabled me to trace this book from Lamport Hall to its present location. I wish also to express my appreciation of the kindness of the

Librarian at Britwell Court, Herbert Collman, Esq., who not only transcribed these poems for me but carefully collated the proof-sheets with the original.

In searching for biographical materials concerning Sir John Salusbury, I was enabled to examine the Cecil Papers at Hatfield House, through the gracious permission of the Marquess of Salisbury, who also gave consent to the reproduction in facsimile of the letter which appears as the frontispiece. In the matter of Salusbury biography, however, my greatest obligation is to A. Foulkes-Roberts, Esq., of Denbigh. Himself a lineal descendant of Catherine of Berain, Mr. Foulkes-Roberts for years has made diligent researches in Salusbury family history. In response to my appeal he cheerfully placed at my disposal the extensive materials which he had collected, including his transcripts from the Bodfari Parish Register and from Robert Parry's Diary. He has also been good enough to read over the section on the Biography of Sir John Salusbury, and thereby has saved me from a number of errors of detail.

C. B.

BRYN MAWR, PA., *October* 1913.

FOREWORD TO THE EARLY ENGLISH TEXT SOCIETY EDITION

THE present volume has already been issued as No. XIV of the Bryn Mawr College Monographs, published and copyrighted by Bryn Mawr College in 1913. While this edition was passing through the press the Directors of the Early English Text Society suggested to me the desirability of giving wider circulation to this Salusbury-Chester material by re-issuing it as one of their publications, and it is with much satisfaction that I avail myself of their offer. I wish at the same time to record my appreciation of the generous action of the authorities of Bryn Mawr College in permitting the re-publication of the volume.

To the list of contents of Christ Church MS. 184 (see below, pp. xxx–xxxvi) should be added the following description of the volume, which has kindly been furnished by Mr. John Munro: 'The manuscript is of paper (195 mm. × 295 mm.), and consists of 302 leaves, besides seven blank leaves of modern paper which have been bound in at the beginning of the book.'

Since the appearance of the earlier edition the Christ Church poems have been again collated with the manuscript by Professor G. C. Moore Smith, who has most generously placed his collations at my disposal. By this means I have been enabled to eliminate a number of errors which stood in the former edition.

C. B.

BRYN MAWR, PA., *March* 1914.

CONTENTS

	PAGE
FOREWORDS	iii
FOREWORD TO THE EARLY ENGLISH SOCIETY TEXT EDITION	v
INTRODUCTION	ix
I. The Biography of Sir John Salusbury .	xi
II. The Contents of the Christ Church Manuscripts	xxvii
III. The Salusbury Poems in the Parry Volume	xl
IV. Who was Robert Chester ? . . .	xlvii
V. The Allegory in *Loves Martyr* . . .	liv
POEMS BY SALUSBURY, CHESTER, AND OTHERS, IN CHRIST CHURCH MS. 184. .	1
POEMS BY SALUSBURY IN THE PARRY VOLUME	45
APPENDIX: A Complaint Addressed to Queen Elizabeth by Sir John Salusbury in the 44th Year of Her Reign	81

LIST OF ILLUSTRATIONS

Facsimile of a Letter from Sir John Salusbury preserved at Hatfield House (Cecil Papers, Vol. 183, No. 67) . . . . . . Frontispiece

Facsimile of fol. 47ª of Christ Church MS. 184

To face p. xxxvii

Facsimiles of Three 'Robert Chester' Signatures

To face p. li

INTRODUCTION

THE interpretation of Shakspere's *Phoenix and Turtle* has occasioned so much difficulty that the perplexed commentator sometimes feels tempted, 'for these dead Birds,' not to 'sigh a prayer' but to breathe a malediction. Shakspere's brief poem in itself presents a hopeless enigma. The allegory of the Phoenix and the Turtle should not, however, be studied in the light of Shakspere's poem alone. If one is to discover its application one must examine also the other 'poeticall essaies' among which Shakspere's lines are included, and above all one must seek the solution of the allegory in Robert Chester's poem, *Loves Martyr*, to which the pieces by Shakspere, Marston, Chapman, Jonson and 'Ignoto' are appended. The close relationship between these supplementary poems and *Loves Martyr* is stated in unmistakable terms on the title-page by which they are introduced:

<blockquote>
Hereafter
follow Diverse
Poeticall Essaies on the former Subject viz. the *Turtle* and *Phoenix*.
</blockquote>

These words suggest, if they do not explicitly affirm, that the allegory in the supplementary pieces merely continues that which is woven into the fabric of *Loves Martyr*. A further consideration pointing in the same direction is the fact that Chester's poem and the supplementary pieces are dedicated to the same patron—Sir John Salusbury of Lleweni.

Such being the case, it would appear that the most promising approach to an understanding of Shakspere's *Phoenix and Turtle* must begin with inquiries concerning Robert Chester, whose poem supplied the basis of the allegory, and Sir John Salusbury, to whom the whole collection of poems is dedicated. Indeed, Professor Gollancz, in a notably judicious statement of the problem, intimates that Salusbury may be not only the patron but also one of the central figures in the allegory. After expressing his confidence, that the solution 'will some day be discovered', he adds this suggestion: 'It would seem from the title-page that the private family history of Sir John Salisbury ought to yield the necessary clue to the events.'[1] In any case it becomes clear that we need to assemble all possible evidence which may throw light upon the personal relations between Chester and Salusbury or between Salusbury and the other poets who dedicated their verses to him.

In the thirty-five years since Dr. Grosart reprinted the 1601 edition of *Loves Martyr*, with a copious Introduction, no further contribution has been made to our information concerning either Robert Chester or his patron. The former Dr. Grosart sought to identify with Sir Robert Chester of Royston, Herts. This identification, which was based purely upon conjecture, must now be abandoned for reasons which will be presented in a later section. In the case of the patron of the poem, Sir John Salusbury, Dr. Grosart was more fortunate. He had no difficulty in identifying him as a young Knight of prominent family whose seat was at Lleweni in Denbighshire. He also pointed out the interesting fact that to the same patron 'Robert Parry Gent.' dedicated in 1597 a small volume of verse which bears the cryptic title: *Sinetes Passions*.

The larger part of Dr. Grosart's Introduction, unfortunately, was devoted to an attempt to prove that the Phoenix and Turtle were, respectively, Elizabeth and the Earl of Essex. This interpretation of the allegory was at the most

---

[1] *The Larger Temple Shakespeare*, vol. xii (1904), Preface to *The Rape of Lucrece*, &c.

a bold guess and is now definitely disproved by the discovery, as will appear later, that Sir John Salusbury was bitterly opposed to the party of Essex, and therefore was the last person to whom such an allegory as Dr. Grosart constructed would have been dedicated. Despite his unsuccessful attempt to interpret the allegory, Dr. Grosart's researches made a valuable contribution to our knowledge concerning *Loves Martyr* and its appended poems, and the materials—both biographical and bibliographical—which he brought together are the basis upon which subsequent critics and commentators have built.

In the following pages two documents are for the first time presented which contain important additional information concerning both Robert Chester and Sir John Salusbury. The first of these is a manuscript preserved in the library of Christ Church, Oxford. The second is a reprint from Robert Parry's volume already mentioned, of that portion which is described on a separate title-page as 'The Patrone his pathetical Posies', &c. These two documents together afford us a series of poems by Salusbury and Chester, many of them signed and dated, and nearly all of them composed prior to the publication of *Loves Martyr*.

Before proceeding to consider these documents, however, it will be well to set down in order the data which I have collected concerning the life and family history of Sir John Salusbury. By availing myself of unprinted materials—especially those at Hatfield House and the Public Record Office—I have been able considerably to enlarge (and in some points to correct) the biographical sketch given by Dr. Grosart (pp. xi–xiii).

I. THE BIOGRAPHY OF SIR JOHN SALUSBURY

Sir John Salusbury of Lleweni—known as 'the Strong'—was the grandson of Sir John Salusbury, Knt., who represented the County of Denbigh in several parliaments and who was appointed constable of Denbigh Castle by Henry VIII in 1530, and held the office of Receiver of North Wales. The bodies of Sir John's grandparents rest in an alabaster tomb in the old Whit-church at Denbigh, surmounted with their effigies; around the side of the tomb are ranged effigies of their nine sons—the second, Robert, in a doctor's gown—and their four daughters—two of the latter being bound in shrouds. The inscription on the tomb reads: 'Here lieth the bodies of Sir Ihon Salusbury of lleweny in the Countie of dēbigh knight: who deceassed the xviijth of march in the yere of our lord God 1578 and dame iane his wief daughter and Co heier to dauid Midleton esquier aldermā of westchester wch iane in A°. 1588 at her charges fully Erected this tombe or Monument & died: the . . . . of . . . . in A°. 15 . . .'[1]

The eldest son of this pair was John Salusbury, Esq., who married Catherine of Berain, and by her had two sons, Thomas and John, and a daughter, Elizabeth.[2] Since John Salusbury, Esq., died in May or June, 1566,[3] his younger son—*our* Sir John Salusbury—was evidently a posthumous child, for he was born probably either in December, 1566, or January, 1567.[4]

---

[1] The will of the elder Sir John Salusbury, dated 1578, was proved in the Prerogative Court of Canterbury, and is now preserved in Somerset House (26 Langley).

[2] Elizabeth Salusbury married Owen Brereton of Borasham, co. Denbigh, who was High Sheriff of the County in 1581 and 1588.

[3] The exact date of his death is not known, but his will (of which a copy is preserved in the St. Asaph District Probate Registry) is dated May 10, 1566; and the probate endorsement bears date July 24 of the same year. I am under obligations to A. Foulkes-Roberts, Esq., of Denbigh, for information concerning this will and for kindly furnishing me with a transcript of it.

[4] An earlier date is excluded by the matriculation record at Jesus College, Nov. 24, 1581, which gives his age as 14 (Foster's *Alumni Oxonienses*, p. 1304). Confirmatory testimony as to the date of his birth is supplied by a portrait of him dated '1591 *aet.* 24' (Pennant's *Tours in Wales*, ed. J. Rhys, Carnarvon, 1883, ii, 140). This latter piece of evidence has already been noted by Dr. Grosart (p. xii).

Introduction

On his mother's side Sir John Salusbury traced his descent from blood royal. Catherine of Berain was the granddaughter of Sir Roland Velville, illegitimate son of Henry VII,[1] and inherited in her own name the Tudor patrimony, 'Penmynydd,' in Anglesey. According to Mrs. Thrale—who was herself a direct descendant of Sir John Salusbury—Catherine of Berain was a ward to Queen Elizabeth and was married to Salusbury by the special consent of her Majesty.[2] In May, 1567, nearly a year after the death of her first husband, Catherine was married to Sir Richard Clough, Knight of the Sepulchre and factor to Queen Elizabeth, who was reputed to be the wealthiest commoner in England.[3]

The three years of her married life with Sir Richard, Catherine spent for the most part in foreign travels. By her second husband she had two daughters, Anne born in 1568 and Mary in 1569. On the death of Sir Richard at Hamburg in 1570, Catherine returned home and shortly after took as her third husband Morris Wyn of Gwydir, Esq., who served three terms as Sheriff of Caernarvonshire and repeatedly represented this county in parliament.[4] Of this union two children were born, Edward and Jane. Morris

---

[1] The line of descent is as follows:

Sir Roland Velville = Agnes Griffith
|
Jane Velville = Tudor ap Robert Vychan
|
Catherine of Berain.

[2] Mrs. Hester L. Piozzi (Mrs. Thrale), *Autobiog. Memoirs*, &c., London, 1861, i. 240. In stating, further, that Catherine's marriage took place in her fifteenth year, Mrs. Thrale is clearly mistaken, for as Catherine was born in 1535 (see below) she must have been 23 years of age when Elizabeth came to the throne.

[3] For an account of Sir Richard Clough see Fuller's *Worthies of England*, ed. 1811, ii. 594; Pennant's *Tours in Wales*, ed. J. Rhys, ii. 136–8; Mrs. Piozzi, *Retrospection*, London, 1801, ii. 155 note. In a 'List of Benefactors' on a tablet in the old Whit-church, Denbigh, is recorded a bequest of £200 by Sir Richard toward the maintenance of a free grammar-school.

[4] See Sir John Wynne, Knt. and Bart., *History of the Gwydir Family*, Oswestry, 1878.

Wyn died August 10, 1580, and his widow was led to the altar for the fourth and last time by Edward Thelwall,[1] of Plas-y-Ward, Denbighshire, who was Sheriff of this County in 1590.[2] Finally, Catherine of Berain—'Mam Cymru' as she has often been styled—died on the 27th of August, 1591, at the age of fifty-six,[3] and was buried beside her first husband in the parish church at Llannefydd. Catherine was long remembered in Wales, and became the subject of more than one picturesque though apocryphal tale. One of these, which has circulated widely, is the amusing anecdote, first printed by Pennant,[4] of her accepting Sir Richard Clough's proposal of marriage while on her way to her first husband's funeral—to the great disappointment of Morris Wyn, who postponed his proposal until the return from the funeral. This story, however, may now be set aside on chronological grounds: Sir Richard's wooing took place in the latter part of April, 1567, when Catherine had already been a widow some eleven months. The numerous poets who celebrated her memory agree in laying stress upon her generous nature and her charitable deeds. Several portraits of her are still in existence,[5] and these

[1] The date of this marriage I have not been able to ascertain, but Catherine was addressed as 'Mrs. Thelwall' in 1586 (see below, p. 36).

[2] Cf. *Hist. MSS. Com.*, Report on Welsh MSS., i. 799. For further information concerning the Thelwall family history see Dwnn's *Heraldic Visitations of Wales*, ed. S. R. Meyrick, ii. 214, 336, and *Archaeologia Cambrensis*, Fifth Series, vii. 314-15. Lord Herbert of Cherbury, who as a boy of nine was placed under Thelwall's charge in the year 1592 in order to learn the Welsh language, has paid high tribute to his personal qualities (*Life of Edward, Lord Herbert*, ed. H. Walpole, 1764, p. 24). Thelwall died July 28, 1610.

[3] 'Vixit sex decies, si demas quattuor annos'—see below, p. 39.

[4] *Tours in Wales*, ed. J. Rhys, ii. 142.

[5] Not all of those which are claimed as her portraits are authentic. One, undoubtedly genuine, which bears the date 1568, is now in the possession of Mr. R. J. Ll. Price of Rhiwlas, and has recently been reproduced in Rev. S. Baring-Gould's *Book of North Wales*, 1903, p. 146. The portrait in Philip Yorke's *Royal Tribes of Wales* (p. 93) can scarcely be a likeness of the same person. Another, which shows her as an old woman, is at present at Wygfair, in the possession of Col. Howard.

Introduction

show her as a woman of strong character and unusual beauty.

In regard to Sir John Salusbury's early years we have little information. At the age of fourteen he went up to Oxford, where he matriculated at Jesus College, Nov. 14, 1581.[1] The records do not show how long he remained at the University or whether he received his degree. Five years after his matriculation at Oxford a tragic event occurred which deeply affected him. His elder brother Thomas was arrested for complicity in the Babington plot, and on Sept. 21, 1586, was executed.[2] In his confession made upon the scaffold Thomas Salusbury made avowal of his religion: 'I have lyved a catholique, and so will I dye.'[3] From this fact one might be led to suspect that the Salusbury family belonged to the Catholic party, but so far as Sir John is concerned there is conclusive evidence, which will be cited later, that he did not share his brother's religion.

As Thomas Salusbury left no male issue, his brother John became thenceforth the heir of Lleweni. Three months later he was united in marriage with Ursula Stanley, natural daughter of Henry Stanley, fourth Earl of Derby, by Jane Halsall of Knowsley, Lancashire.[4] Though of illegitimate birth, it is to be noted that Salusbury's wife was an acknowledged child and bore her father's surname.

In the Registers of Bodfari parish—near the limits of which Lleweni is situated—one finds recorded the baptisms of the children born to Sir John and his wife. As these entries are of importance for our purpose, I quote them in

[1] Foster's *Alumni Oxonienses*, p. 1304.

[2] For an account of the trial of Salusbury and the other conspirators see Thos. B. Howell, *Collection of State Trials*, i. 1127 ff.

[3] *Hist. MSS. Com.*, Report xiv, App., part iv, p. 614.

[4] See the *Victorian Co. Hist. of Lancashire*, iii. 162, note 10: 'By Jane Halsall, of Knowsley, he [the Earl of Derby] had several natural children— Thomas Stanley of Eccleshall and Broughton in Salford, Dorothy, wife of Sir Cuthbert Halsall, and Ursula, wife of Sir John Salusbury—for whom he made liberal provision.'

xvi *Poems by Sir John Salusbury and Robert Chester*

full from a transcript made by A. Foulkes-Roberts, Esq., of Denbigh, which he most kindly placed at my disposal.

Jane Salusbury, Daughter to John Salusbury Esquier and heire of lleweny was baptized the xth daye of October [1587].

Harry Salusbury sonne to John Salusbury Esquier heire of lleweny was baptized the xxvjth of October, died the same day & was buried the next daye after at Whytchurch by Denbighe [1588].

Harry Salusbury sonne to John Salusbury Esquier and heir of lleweny was baptized the xxiiijth daye of September [1589]. *The said Harry Salusberi was confirmed at the house of lleweni by the bus^{h}ppe of Bangor upone michells daye* 1591 *Mr Willm Almor beinge his godfather.*[1]

Ihon Salusbury sonne to Mr Iohn Salusbury Esquier and heir of lleweny was baptized & buried at Whitechurche the xxvijth day of July [1590].

Iohn Salusbury sonne to Mr John Salusbury heyre of lleweny Esquier was baptized the viijth of November and was born the thyrd day of the same moneth [1592].

ffrancis Salusbury sonne to Mr John Salusbury heire of Lleweny Esquier was baptized the viijth of Aprill and was buried the next day folowinge at the white Churche [1594].

Wiliam Salusbury sonne to John Salusbury Esquier & heire of Llewenye was Baptized the vijth of Maye and was confirmed by the Lorde bushop of St. assaphe at Place in llewyny upon the xviijth daye of June next folowinge [1595].

Oriana daughter to Mr John Salusbury of llewenye Esqui' was baptized the vjth day of June [1597].

[2] Velivel Salusbury sonne to John Salusbury of lleweny es & to Grace Peake was baptized the xxvjth of October [1597].

Fardynando Salusbury the 4 sonne of John Salusbury of lleweny Esquiere was borne upon thyrsday the 3 of maie aboute 4 of the Clocke in the morninge of the same Daye, & Christened upon Mondaye after, whose godfathers were Michaell Othen D: in Phisicke & Mr Harry Williams of Cochwillan gent & his godmother was M^{ries} Margrett of Penporchell [1599].

David Salusbury the sonne of John Salusbury of lleweny Esquier was borne upon Thuesday the 19 of August about 2 of the Clocke in the astor Dinn' and was baptized upon thyrsday the 28 of the same moneth whose godfathers were David Holland Esquier & Cadwaladr Wyn' gent' and Anne Cloughe the wife of Roger Sa: of Bachegrege Esqr. godmother. The said David Sa: died and was buried at Whitchurch upon thuesday the 16 of ffebruary following [1600].

In March, 1593, while in the city of Chester, Sir John was engaged in a serious affray with one Owen Salusbury,

[1] The sentence in italics has been interlined afterwards.

[2] An asterisk is placed opposite this name in the register to denote illegitimacy.

Introduction

in which the latter was so grievously wounded that at first it was feared he might not survive. Sir John's father-in-law, the Earl of Derby, wrote from London to the Mayor of Chester, directing that the best surgical aid should be procured for the wounded man, and that in case of his death judicial inquiry be made into the affair.[1] Meanwhile Sir John had fled to avoid arrest and found refuge at the house of ' Mr. Trevors of Trevallen '[2]—apparently the same person as the Sir Richard Trevor who a few years later appears as his implacable enemy. As to the causes which provoked this encounter we are left in ignorance. It may be noted that the wounded combatant recovered, and that, as Captain Owen Salusbury, he is frequently mentioned among the most active partisans of the Earl of Essex.[3] He appears to have met his death at Essex House, London, while serving his master's cause in the ill-fated rising.[4]

[1] This letter is preserved among the MSS. of the Corporation of Chester, *Hist. MSS. Com.*, Report viii, App., part i, 375, col. 1. One receives the impression that Owen Salusbury was a chronically contentious person from two letters which he addressed to Sir Francis Walsingham some three years before the affray at Chester. Nov. 18, 1589, he wrote to ask assistance in securing pardon for himself and others (*Calendar of Domestic Papers*, 1581-1590, p. 630). In 1590 he complained that he had been abused by one Cosby, who would not meet him, though he had challenged him (Lansdowne MS. 99, Art. 95).

[2] *Hist. MSS. Com.*, *ibid.*, p. 375, col. 2.

[3] In a letter dated June 10, 1597, Capt. Owen Salusbury is stated to have received 150 trained soldiers from Herefordshire (*Hist. MSS. Com.*, Report on MSS. at Hatfield House, Part vii, 250). His name appears in lists of the officers who served in Ireland, under Essex (*ibid.*, part ix, 146 and 330). After Essex's return to England, Capt. Owen Salusbury is frequently mentioned as one of his trusted lieutenants (*ibid.*, part xi, 42, 96 and 103) and his movements were closely watched by Government informers shortly before the Essex rising.

[4] MS. Diary of Robert Parry, in possession of Col. T. A. Wynne Edwards of Plâs Nantglyn, p. 52 : ' In this conflyct in the howse [i. e. Essex House] was slaye wth a peece frō the street Capt. Owen Salusburie & one or two more hurte & some hurte & kylled in the street.' For this and the following quotations from Parry's diary I am indebted to the kindness of A. Foulkes-Roberts, Esq., of Denbigh, who has transcribed the document with the intention of publishing it. The death of Owen Salusbury is also mentioned in a contemporary account of the Essex rising printed by J. J. Munro, *Athenaeum*, Dec. 26, 1908, p. 820.

Two years after the affray at Chester, we find Sir John Salusbury at London, and it is with London quite as much as with North Wales that the next ten years of his life are connected. On coming up to the city he was admitted March 19, 1594–5, as a student of the Middle Temple.[1] In the same month he was also appointed one of the Esquires of the body to the Queen.[2] On April 13, 1597, he was appointed by the Privy Council Deputy Lieutenant for the County of Denbigh, in place of Gilbert Gerrard deceased. It is interesting to note that Salusbury had been recommended for this appointment by Sir Philip Sidney's brother-in-law, the Earl of Pembroke, who was at that time Lord President of Wales.[3] During these years Salusbury seems to have continued to enjoy the favour of the Queen: he held his office as one of the Queen's men down to the time of her death, and in June, 1601, he was knighted by Elizabeth's own hand.[4]

This year, 1601—the very year which Robert Chester and the group of greater Elizabethans dedicated their poems to him—marks the zenith in Sir John Salusbury's fortunes. Indeed, before the close of the year, we find him attacked by a circle of enemies in Denbighshire, whose hostility at length drove him from the Court and embittered the remaining

[1] Hopwood, *Middle Temple Records*, i. 351, among the admissions of March 19: 'John Salisbury of Llawenny Denbighshire, esq., specially; with assent of Mr. Pagitt and other Masters of the Bench.'

[2] MS. Diary of Robert Parry.

[3] The following is an extract from the letter of appointment, addressed by the Privy Council to the Lord Keeper [Sir Thomas Egerton]: '... and therefore his Lordship [the Earl of Pembroke] hathe recomended unto us John Salsbury of Lleweney, esquire, to be a gentleman of good livlyhoode and by longe continuance of his auncestours well esteemed in the country and also her Majesty's servant, and one his Lordship doth thincke worthie the credite of the place' (*Acts of the Privy Council*, 1597, p. 39).

[4] MS. Diary of Robert Parry, p. 54: 'In June Mr John Salusburie of lleweny beinge before sworne to be the Queens man was by her ma^{tie}: knighted.' See also the record of fees paid by Salusbury in connexion with this ceremony, Christ Church MS. 184, fol. 49^b, as described below. It is singular that Sir John's name is omitted by Metcalfe, *Book of Knights*, and also by W. A. Shaw, *Knights of England* (1906).

Introduction

years of his life. In September, 1601, the Queen sent to the High Sheriff of Denbighshire a writ directing that at the next County Court a knight and burgess should be chosen to represent the county in Parliament. At the same time Sir John Salusbury signified his intention of standing for election as knight of the shire. This was the signal for active plotting on the part of Sir John's enemies to prevent him from realizing his ambition. The leaders in this hostile movement were Sir John Lloyd of Llanrhayader and his brothers-in-law, Sir Richard Trevor of Trevallyn and Capt. John Salusbury, together with Thomas Trafford, Esq., of Treffordd in Esclusham. Their unfriendliness toward Salusbury probably had its origin in some neighbourhood feud, though it may have been aggravated by political differences. Lloyd and Capt. Salusbury, at least, had been conspicuous among the adherents of Essex.[1] After the fall of Essex Capt. Salusbury was arrested and imprisoned for several months for his part in the rebellion. He wrote repeatedly to Cecil imploring forgiveness for his error,[2] and at length was released on payment of a fine of £40.[3] Quite aside from political controversies, however, there is abundant evidence of strained relations for several years previous between Sir Richard Trevor, Sir John Lloyd, and Capt. Salusbury on the one hand, and the Thelwalls, with whom Sir John Salusbury was allied by his mother's fourth marriage,[4] on the other hand.

[1] See the 'Information concerning Sir John Lloyd' and others, *Hist. MSS. Com.*, Report on MSS. at Hatfield House, Part xi, p. 96; in a letter dated Feb. 11, 1600-1, concerning the Essex conspirators, Capt. John Salusbury is mentioned as one of 'these principal traitors' (*ibid.*, pp. 42-3).

[2] Letters dated July 16, 20, and 28, 1601 (*Hist. MSS. Com.*, Report on MSS. at Hatfield House, part xi, pp. 287, 294, and 307).

[3] *Ibid.*, p. 214.

[4] Sir Richard Trevor had made complaint to the Star Chamber of riotous and violent actions committed by Edward Thelwall on Nov. 28, 1590. (Star Chamber Proceedings, Public Record Office, Elizabeth T$\frac{19}{32}$ and T$\frac{37}{17}$.) In 1598, as appears from a letter written by Francis Bacon to the Secretary of Essex, one of the Thelwalls, a mercer, had caused the arrest of Capt. Salusbury for a debt of 100 marks (*Hist. MSS.*

Whatever the cause, there is no doubt that for several years before 1601 Sir John had been involved in animosities with some of the influential gentry of Denbighshire,[1] and that his adversaries now determined to defeat his election to Parliament. In the execution of their designs they were materially assisted by Owen Vaughan, then High Sheriff of the County, who appears to have been the tool of Sir John's enemies. It was arranged that the election should take place not at Denbigh but at Wrexham, in the extreme eastern part of the county, where the adverse sentiment was strongest. The date fixed for the election was Oct. 21. When the day arrived Sir John found the streets of Wrexham patrolled by bands of armed men who had been assembled by his opponents, ostensibly to preserve the peace, but really to overawe the friends of Salusbury. Between 8 and 9 in the morning a clash occurred in the Wrexham churchyard between Sir John's party and the bands of his enemies, and thereupon the Sheriff, using this disorder as a convenient pretext, adjourned the session of the County Court, without holding any election whatever, to the great chagrin and mortification of Sir John, who was confident of receiving

Com., Report on MSS. at Hatfield House, part viii, 355). Charges of extortion and conspiracy were preferred against Sir John Lloyd and Capt. Salusbury before the Star Chamber by Robert Thelwall of Ruthin, near Denbigh, covering acts committed from 1596 to 1600 (Star Chamber Proceedings, Elizabeth T_{3T}^{5} and T_{5}^{34} and T_{44}^{39}). That Sir John Salusbury was directly interested in pressing these charges appears from his letter to Sir Robert Cecil, April 22, 1602, protesting indignantly against a postponement which had been granted to the defendants: 'After my comming into the cuntrey I doe find that my opposites have since complotted to worke an extraordinarie staie of a suite preferred in the Starr chamb' a yeare and a half sithence by one Theleoll against Sr Joen Lloid, Capteyne Joen Salusburie & others of their faccion for redresse of former wronge practised against him, and others, and for sundry heynous oppressions and extorcions vppon the Cuntrey committed by them, by coolour of their former Capteineshipps and offices.' (Printed in substance, *Hist. MSS. Com.*, Report on MSS. at Hatfield House, part xii, 118.)

[1] Read in this connexion Robert Chester's poem, 'A poore sheapheard's profecye' (pp. 20–21 below). The 'limping foxe' there mentioned may have been Trevor or Sir John Lloyd.

a majority of the votes even under these unfavourable conditions.

Our information concerning this affair at Wrexham is derived from accounts of it addressed to Sir Robert Cecil, and also from complaints and cross-complaints made by both parties to the Star Chamber, which undertook an investigation of the matter. The earliest account is that given by Sir John in a letter dispatched to Cecil Oct. 24, only three days after the event. A facsimile reproduction of this letter [1] is presented herewith (see frontispiece); the substance of the letter has been printed by the Historical MSS. Commission.[2] Another letter to Cecil, written by Justice Lewknor a week later,[3] makes brief reference to the 'great disorder' which had broken out in Denbighshire, in terms which are distinctly more judicial. But the most circumstantial account of the affair is to be found in the formal complaint which was addressed to the Queen by Sir John Salusbury.[4] The document, despite its tedious legal verbiage, possesses much interest on account of the lively details which it gives, particularly in the portion describing the assault upon Sir John in the Wrexham churchyard. The reader will find the larger portion of the text of this document in the Appendix.

It may perhaps be suspected that Sir John's account of the affair is not wholly unbiased. He was, we may well believe, too much of a Hotspur to stand so patiently on the defensive as he represents himself as doing. Those who wish to read the other side of the story will find it in the counter-complaint of Sir Richard Trevor against Sir John Salusbury and others.[5] But Trevor's narrative, on the

[1] *Cecil Papers*, vol. 183, no. 67.
[2] Report on MSS. at Hatfield House, part xi, 445-6. It is there stated to be a holograph, but only the signature appears to be in Salusbury's own hand.
[3] Printed in substance, *Hist. MSS. Com.*, *ibid.*, p. 460.
[4] Star Chamber Proceedings, Pub. Rec. Office, 44th year of Eliz., S$\frac{11}{4}$.
[5] Star Chamber Proceedings, Eliz. T $\frac{13}{8}$.

whole, lacks the specific details which make Salusbury's version so convincing. Trevor supplies us with a long list of the supporters of Salusbury which is of interest chiefly to the local historian. The only name in the list which need be noted here is that of 'Richard Parry of Henllan in the County of Denbigh gent.' Richard, who is thus enrolled among Salusbury's friends, was the brother of Robert Parry the poet.

One sentence in Sir Richard Trevor's complaint is important on account of the light which it throws upon the question of Salusbury's attitude towards the Earl of Essex:

... the said Sir John Salusburie sayd that he would take place of your subiect [i.e. Sir Rich. Trevor] & Sr Jhon lloyde or elles he would die for it, & that he held hymself a better man then he that knighted your subiect [1] & that the said Sr Jhon lloyd was knighted by a traytor.

The person at whom this second thrust was aimed is disclosed in an 'Information concerning Sir John Lloyd' and others, dated February, 1600–1, which states that Lloyd had been 'lately knighted in Ireland by the Earl of Essex, whom he followed in the late service there'.[2]

It is not altogether clear what action was taken in regard to the Wrexham riot by the Privy Council. On Nov. 5, 1601, the Council sent identical letters to Sir John Salusbury, Sir Richard Trevor, and Sir John Lloyd, summoning them to the Court without delay to answer to their misdemeanours at the election riot.[3] In the official membership roll of the Parliament of 1601 are entered for Denbighshire the names of Sir John Salusburye, Knt., and John Panton, gent.— both returned '16 Dec. 1601'. This would look as though a second election was ordered shortly after the abortive

[1] Sir Richard Trevor was knighted in the Glynes in 1597 by the Rt. Hon. Sir William Russell, Knt., lord deputy general of Ireland.

[2] *Hist. MSS. Com.*, Report on MSS. at Hatfield House, part xi, 96. The statement in W. A. Shaw's *Knights of England* (1906) that Sir John Lloyd was knighted in Holland by the Earl of Leicester is, accordingly, ncorrect.

[3] *Acts of the Privy Council*, 1601–4, pp. 342–3. In answer to these summons Trevor presented himself Nov. 20, Salusbury Nov. 23, and Lloyd Nov. 24.

Introduction xxiii

election at Wrexham, and that this time Sir John gained his seat. Even if a second election was held it is certain that this did not terminate the inquiry by the Privy Council, for we find a series of depositions in regard to the outrage at Wrexham dated Feb. 20, 1601–2.[1] Though the decision of the Privy Council has not been preserved, a passage in a letter written by Sir John Salusbury [2] suggests that the action which they took was far from satisfactory to him.

The feud in Denbighshire did not end with 1601, but seems rather to have increased in bitterness. On July 7, 1602, John Lewis Gwyn, a kinsman of Sir John Salusbury, was murdered by the partisans of his opponents.[3] Indictments were found by the Grand Jury at the following Michaelmas session against seven persons for this crime, among them being William Lloyd of Foxhall, son of John Lloyd, and also Foulke Lloyd, who ten years before had held the office of High Sheriff and who had been prominent in the attack upon Sir John Salusbury at Wrexham. The accused persons were not without influential friends, and it was openly boasted that pardon would be secured for them. Conspicuous among those who exerted themselves on their behalf was Sir John's old enemy, Captain John Salusbury.[4]

---

[1] 'Examinatio Capt. 20 die ffebruary anno M^{ae} Eliz. etc., 44,' Star Chamber Proceedings, Eliz. T_{31}^{9}. The deponents, who were eye-witnesses of the fray in Wrexham churchyard, give many interesting details. Their testimony is on the side of Salusbury.

[2] Letter to Cecil from Lleweni, April 22, 1602: 'I am bould to acquaint your Lo[rdship] how that albeit I did yeld my self to the Lords, in regard of my alleagiance to her Ma*ie*stie and my dutie to their hono*u*rs, to putt vp and beare w*i*th such private great iniuries donne by my adue*r*saries to me (which I must endure as I may) . . .' (*Cecil Papers*, vol. 92, no. 149, printed in substance, *Hist. MSS. Com.*, Report on MSS. at Hatfield House, part xii, 118.)

[3] The exact date of Gwyn's murder is given in Robert Parry's diary. Parry also supplies the information that William Lloyd of Foxhall, one of the assassins, was the son of John Lloyd.

[4] See Sir John Salusbury's letter to Cecil, Nov. 10, 1602, of which an abstract is printed (*Hist. MSS. Com.*, Report on MSS. at Hatfield House, part xii, 467–8).

Between 1602 and 1604 Sir John wrote repeatedly to Cecil to secure his assistance in bringing to justice the murderers of his kinsman. A passage in one of these letters is of special interest as suggesting that in these factional strifes religious controversies played some part. Sir John declares of Foulke Lloyd, 'that he is a knowne notorious Recusant and a harborer and mainteyner of Iesuites & Seminaries, and is a member evell affected to the state and hath not receaved the Communion theis many yeres.'[1] This statement at the same time proves conclusively that Sir John himself did not share the religion of his unfortunate brother, who was one of the Babington conspirators.

These letters from Salusbury to Cecil exhibit the relations of friendly confidence which existed between them and disclose the fact that Cecil more than once used his influence to protect Salusbury's interests.[2] On the other hand, it is plainly intimated in these letters that some of the Lords of the Privy Council were giving active support to Salusbury's enemies.[3]

In these contentions Sir John Salusbury was involved

[1] *Cecil Papers*, Hatfield House, vol. 108, no. 9. One may refer in this connexion to the letter of Justice Lewknor to Cecil, Oct. 31, 1601, in which he makes mention of the recent activity of the Catholics in Shropshire and the borders of Wales (*Hist. MSS. Com.*, Report on MSS. at Hatfield House, part xi, 460).

[2] 'I received this day', Lord Zouche, President of Wales, wrote to Cecil, Sept. 2, 1602, 'a letter from you concerning Sir John Salsbury. If he will be ordered, I will do him all the kindness I may. It may be, I will go to the Assizes to see if I can make a friendship amongst them in that shire.' (*Hist. MSS. Com.*, Report on MSS. at Hatfield House, part xii, 342.) Salusbury wrote himself to Cecil, Sept. 21, to thank him for his good offices with the Lord President (*ibid.*, p. 391). At another time, as appears from one of Salusbury's letters, Cecil wrote to the Lord Chancellor to secure a stay of the pardon which had been secured for Foulke Lloyd (Letter to Cecil, dated July 20, 1604, *Cecil Papers*, vol. 106, no. 9).

[3] Letter from Sir John Salusbury to Cecil, July 29, 1602: 'I have been informed how some of the Lords are in hand to prefer their own late servants and followers to be the only deputy-lieutenants in this County, viz., Sir John Lloid, with Sir Richard Trevor, his brother-in-law' (*Hist. MSS. Com.*, Report on MSS. at Hatfield House, part xii, 263).

when Elizabeth's reign came to an end. He at once took his departure from London and went down to his home, taking part at Denbigh in the public ceremony proclaiming the new King. It is clear that Sir John regarded his absence from Court as only temporary, and expected to be appointed to some position in the service of King James.[1] But the appointment for which he waited never came, and there is no evidence that he ever returned to London. Moreover, he appears to have been harassed about this time by petty creditors and his enemies eagerly seized upon these embarrassments to discredit him to the King. These new troubles form the subject of a letter to Cecil dated June 26, 1609, which stands as a pathetic conclusion to this correspondence.

'I have bene enformed', he writes, 'that somme Aduersaries of myne (to wreake there malice againste me) have (of late) practized to incence the Kinges moste excellente matie of some disobedience in me to processes in lawe vpon somme matters of Suytes for small dettes, purposinge thereby to procure his hignes indignacion against me. I haue thoughte it meete in most humble maner to aduertize your gracious Lo[rd]ship that I haue offred and am redie to make all reasonable satisfaccions to those that (of meere stomock) do prosecute against me, but nothinge wilbe accepted. And also that God hathe (of late) visited me with extreame Sickness for a longe tyme, both whiche have altogether impeded me from travaile to come and cleere my self of there surmized accusacions, whereby my said aduersaries tuke advantage to aggravate there complaintes againste me. If your Lo[rd]ship do happen to finde that (by there sinister meanes)

[1] In a letter to Cecil dated April 15, 1603, Sir John explains his reasons for returning to Lleweni and signifies his readiness to undertake any employment in the service of the King. 'And not being called vppon by your honor,' he continues, somewhat anxiously it would seem, 'I am at this tyme bowlde to sygnyffy vnto you the contynuance of my dutyffull love towardes your honor, humbly praying your honor that I may heare ffrom you, whyther yt ys your pleasure that I shulde make my repayre to attend your honor' (*Cecil Papers*, vol. 187, no. 29).

his highnes shold be possessed of any harde Opinion of me, my humble desire & peticion is that (by your Lo[rdship's] honorable meanes) there be no further Credit geven to suche my Calumniatours vntill it shall please God to restore vnto me such parte of healthe as I may be able to travell & to purge my self, which shalbe performed as soone as my estate of Body will permitte.'[1]

It does not appear that Sir John ever recovered his health. During the next three years I find no information concerning him, and then comes abruptly the record of his death, which occurred July 24, 1612. For the precise date of his death we are indebted to an entry in the Journal of Peter Roberts of St. Asaph.[2] In his memorandum Roberts adds that, according to report, Sir John's body was buried the same night. But no reference to a nocturnal burial occurs in the entry in the Bodfari Parish Register:

John Salusbury, Knight, heyre of the house of Lleweny was interred & buried in whitchurch vpon St James day, being the .25. day of July [1612].

No record of Sir John's will has been found, but at Somerset House, under date 1619, is recorded the release of certain claims against the estate by two creditors,[3] in which one may see further evidence of the financial difficulties in which he was involved toward the close of his life.

He was survived by his wife Ursula, who apparently did not die until 1636,[4] by one son, Henry, who several years before had followed his father's example in entering the

[1] *Cecil Papers*, vol. 195, no. 106.

[2] *Y Cwtta Cyfarwydd: The Chronicle written by the Famous Clarke, Peter Roberts, notary public, for the years 1607–1646*, &c., London, 1883, p. 35.

[3] Sentences, fol. 116, Parker, 1619: 'Sententia absolutoris in causa [W^m] Davies et [Thos] Johnson contra [Henry] Salisbury.'

[4] See Grosart, p. xii. The statement in Burke's *Peerage* that Ursula Salusbury died in 1591 is clearly an error: see, for example, the reference to Ursula in the lines by Bernard Jones (No. XXV) which bear the date 1596.

Middle Temple,[1] and who was created a baronet Nov. 10, 1619, and by three daughters : (1) Jane, who married Thomas Price of Plas-yolyn, (2) Oriana, who married John Parry of Twysog, (3) Arabella, who married John Johnes of Halkyn.[2]

II. THE CONTENTS OF THE CHRIST CHURCH MANUSCRIPTS

In the library of Christ Church, Oxford, are preserved two MSS.—Nos. 183 and 184—which were evidently at one time the property of the Salusburys of Lleweni. The major portion of the contents of either volume consists of Welsh verse composed by various bards in praise of members of the Salusbury family. An examination of the names and dates of these poems shows that all of them were written within the lifetime of Sir John Salusbury—and many of them were composed in his honour. In addition to this Welsh poetry these volumes contain a considerable body of material in English : copies of letters, medical recipes, and finally—what is of special interest to us—a series of English poems. Practically all of this English material is contemporary with Sir John Salusbury—the sole exception being the copy, in MS. 183, of a letter from Charles I, dated 1625.

I present herewith a list of the contents of these two manuscripts.

Christ Church MS. 183.

fol. 3–4.   Two leaves printed on one side only, on which an early hand has written the date 1596.

fol. 3^b.   ' Sundrie necessarie obseruations, meete for a Christian ' ; in prose, 21 points in all.

fol. 4^a.   A printed poem of 30 lines entitled : ' Certaine necessarie obseruations for Health ' [= No. XX in MS. 184].

[1] He was admitted Nov. 27, 1607 ; see Hopwood, *Middle Temple Records*, ii, 486.
[2] Burke's *Peerage*, London, 1862, p. 935.

fol. 5ª.	Apothecaries' weights and measures.
fol. 5ᵇ.	'The explication of all the weights and measures which commonly are vsed in Phisicke.'
fol. 6ª–8ᵇ.	'Certaine receites for my Honorable good freinde Sʳ John Salusbury knight.'
fol. 9ª	(in another hand). A recipe for an oil which will heal any wound however dangerous, 'sent by Gabriell Dennys from Rome.' At the foot of the page: 'Sic vale, George Stanley.' [See also Christ Church MS. 184, fol. 79.]
fol. 9ᵇ–11ᵇ.	More recipes, for various ills.
fol. 12ª.	Copy of a letter by 'Sʳ Henry Sydney, knight of the order and Lord President of Wales, & then Lord deputie of Ireland, wrytinge to his yonge sonne Mʳ Phē Sydney.'
fol. 12ᵇ.	A shorter letter from 'The Ladie marie Sydney' to the same.
fol. 13ª.	Copy of 'A letter of the Lorde Keapers to the Earle of Essex, Earle Marshall of Englande'.
fol. 13ᵇ–14ᵇ.	(wrongly numbered 15). The Earl of Essex's reply.
fol. 15ᵇ.	Copies of two letters by Sir Walter Raleigh, (1) to King James; (2) to Sir Robert Carre.
fol. 16ᵇ.	Copy of a letter from Charles I, dated Aug. 13, 1625. Inc.: 'Right trusty and right beloved Cousin we greete you well.'
fol. 17.	More recipes.
fol. 18–19.	Blank.

Here follows a series of seven Welsh poems, each one headed: 'Moliant Sion Salusburi Escwiair wy'r ac aer Sʳ Shion Salusburi Marchog vrddol o Leweni a Siamberlen gwynedd,' i.e.: In praise of John Salusbury Esquire, grandson and heir of Sir John Salusbury of Lleweni, worthy Knight, and Receiver of North Wales.

fol. 20^a.	(1) By Simwnt Vachan.
fol. 21^a.	(2) By Shion Mawddwy, dated April 15, 1593.
fol. 22^b.	(3) By Shion Tudur, dated 'Myhelm 3, 1593'.
fol. 23^b.	(4) By Huw Machno, dated as the preceding.
fol. 24^b.	(5) By Wiliam Cynwal.
fol. 25^b.	(6) By John Phylyp.
fol. 26^b.	(7) By Robert Ilan.
fol. 27^b–92^b.	Blank.

The leaves which follow are numbered in a new series, beginning with 1.

fol. 8^b.	The Salusbury crest, surmounted with the motto : 'Posse et nolle nobile.'
fol. 9^a.	Sir John Salusbury's arms marshalled, with separate figures of a Saracen's head and a lion's head in the upper corners of the page. Beneath the arms is a scroll with the motto : 'Posse et nolle nobile.'
fol. 9^b–20^b.	Blank.
fol. 21.	Copy of a letter, 'To ye right honourable Charles, Earle of Notingham,' &c. It relates to Newfoundland.
fol. 22^a–28^b.	Blank.

A series of Welsh poems, in praise of Sir John Salusbury of Lleweni, except as otherwise stated :

fol. 29^a.	By Gruffyd Hafren.
fol. 31^a.	By Huw Machno.
fol. 33^a.	By Ed. Wienn (a half-brother of Sir John Salusbury).
fol. 35^b.	By 'H. Ph.'
fol. 37^a.	By Sion Evans, in praise of Henry son of Sir John Salusbury. At the end is the date, Christmas 1607 ; on the margin has been written : 'xx^o decembris A^o salutis 1608.'

xxx *Poems by Sir John Salusbury and Robert Chester*

fol. 39^b.	By R. Kyffin, dated Christmas, 1607.
fol. 41^a.	By Thomas Pennllyn, dated as the preceding.
fol. 42^b.	By Sion Kain, dated as the preceding.
fol. 44^a.	By Gruffydd Hafrenn, dated as the preceding.
fol. 46^a.	By Robert llyn, dated as the preceding.
fol. 47^b.	By Richard Phillip, dated Easter, 1608.
fol. 49^b.	By Huw Pennant, dated Christmas.
fol. 51^a.	By Rys Kain, in praise of Mr Harry Salusbury, son and heir of Sir John Salusbury Knight; dated 1608.
fol. 52^b.	By Sion Kain.
fol. 54^b.	By 'H. Ph.'
fol. 56^a.	By Sion Kain, in praise of Sir Harry Salusbury of Lleweni, Knight and Baronet.
fol. 57^b.	By Sion Kain; an elegy upon Mr John Salusbury second son of Sir John Salusbury, Knight.
fol. 59^b.	Blank.
fol. 60^a.	By Sion Kain; an elegy upon Mr Ferdinando Salusbury, fourth son of Sir John Salusbury of Lleweni, Knight.
fol. 61^b–71^b.	Blank.
fol. 72^a.	Welsh verses without heading; at the end (fol. 73^a) stands the name, 'Sion Cain.'
fol. 73^a.	Eight lines of Welsh verse by 'Rees ap Iohn'.
fol. 73^b.	'An Englishe Copie of the pardon granted by Kinge James, 24 July A° primo of his Raigne of England, 1603.'
fol. 76^b.	Copy of a legal document dated 15th of Henry VIII, relating to a mill at Esclusham.
fol. 78^b	(wrongly numbered 77). A few lines of Welsh verse over the name 'Wliam nathe'.

Christ Church MS. 184.

fol. i–ii.	Fly-leaves containing much scribbling, some of it in Sir John Salusbury's hand. On fol. i^b occurs this distich:

Introduction

<blockquote>
Who seeketh other men to insnare
nets for him selfe he doth prepare
finis J. S.
</blockquote>

On the same page are eight lines of Welsh verse subscribed 'finis Thomas lewis', and two Welsh quatrains by 'Mistres bankes'. On fol. ii are scraps of Welsh verse subscribed: 'hugh ap Wylliam', 'hughe machin', 'J. T.' (i.e. John Tudder of Llannefydd), 'William Kynwal', 'John Mowthwy', 'Hughe llivon'.

fol. 1.   The title-page in Welsh in the hand of William Kynwal.[1]

fol. 1^b.   Following eight lines of Welsh verse, two English quatrains:

<blockquote>
I Count his quonquest great
that Cann by reson stil
Subdu affexions his heat
and bridel wanton will.
                  J. S. [in Salusbury's hand]
</blockquote>

<blockquote>
I woulde I once might see in you
such reason for to raingne
wch conquer myght your Apetite
booth winn you fame and gayne.
        finis V. S. [Vrsula Salusbury ?]
</blockquote>

fol. 2.   Here begins the Pedigree of Catharine of Berain, in Welsh, written by William Kynwal of Penmachno.

Following the pedigree are various recipes, &c.

fol. 22^a.   On the top margin, a Latin distich partly trimmed away by the binder, and an English paraphrase:

<blockquote>
furst stop the cause too late doth phisick come
When euills small to great (by sufferance) runne.
        finis J. Salusbury 1592.
</blockquote>

fol. 34–35.   English poems; text printed—Nos. I and II.

[1] See below, the description of fol. 89–174.

xxxii *Poems by Sir John Salusbury and Robert Chester*

fol. 36–38.　　　Medical recipes.
fol. 39ª.　　　　Titles of three documents among the Patent Rolls of Henry VII, relating to official appointments held by Salusbury's ancestors.
fol. 40.　　　　Verses by Ben Jonson (holograph)—No. III.
fol. 41ª.　　　　Verses (in Robert Chester's hand ?)—No. IV.
fol. 42ª.　　　　The arms of Sir John Salusbury marshalled, with his monogram above and a scroll below bearing the motto : 'Nī thry Angaù fy medawl. J. S.' The meaning of the motto seems to be : Death does not turn aside my purpose.
fol. 43ª–49ª.　　Poems, the most of them by Robert Chester ; text printed—Nos. V–XIX.
fol. 49ʰ.　　　　'ffees due to be paid by all Knight*es* made by he^r ma^{tie} Q. to the officers of her ma^{ties} chamb^r as followeth this note being laid downe by m^r Braconburie & m^r Conwey gentleme*n* vshers, and paid to their hand*es* for all by Sr John Salusburie, Knight, 1601.' The sum total is £11 13*s*. 4*d*. At the foot is Salusbury's autograph. On the lower portion of the page, in the same hand, are written verses of Scripture in English, viz.: *Prov*. 25: 26–28 ; 26: 4–5.

Here follows a series of Welsh poems all addressed to Sir John Salusbury except as otherwise noted :

fol. 51.　　　　Kowydd (i.e. poem) by Thomas Penllyn.
fol. 53.　　　　Kowydd by Rhys Dwnn.
fol. 54.　　　　Kowydd, to the sons of Sir John Salusbury, by Rhys Dwnn.
fol. 56–57　　　(two inserted leaves). Kowydd, to Jesus Christ, by David Llwyd Mothe.
fol. 58.　　　　An imperfect poem, dated 1602.
fol. 60.　　　　Kowydd by Richard Philip.
fol. 61.　　　　Awdl (i.e. ode) by Elis Rhydderch, dated 1602.

fol. 63.	Kowydd by Dafydd Goch.
fol. 64.	Kowydd by Gruffyd Hafren.
fol. 66.	Awdl by Sion Mawddn.
fol. 67.	Kowydd by Morus Berwyn.
fol. 69.	Awdl by 'Gr. Rh.'
fol. 70.	Kowydd by Simwnt Vychan.
fol. 72.	Kowydd by the same.
fol. 74.	Kowydd by Robert Evans.
fol. 77^b.	An English poem in beautiful lettering by a professional scribe, with Salusbury's autograph at the top—No. XX. At the bottom of the page several proverbs of Solomon in Salusbury's hand.
fol. 78^b.	Covered with scribbled rhymes in several hands, among them being Salusbury's. The following lines are in the same hand which wrote Nos. XXVI, XXVIII, and XXIX :

> all is hazard that we have
> there is nothinge bidinge
> dayes of pleasures at [sic] but stremes,
> through faire medowes s[liding]
> weale or woe time doth goe
> in tyme no returninge
> secrete fates giudes [sic] our states,
> both in mirth & moorninge.

fol. 79^a.	'An oyle of Aparisio, a Spanyard which hadd of the Kinge a verrie greate pension, to hym and his wyfe for inventinge the same, to heale any wounde, be it neuer so daungerous. Sent by Gabriell Dennys from Rome.' Signed at the end: 'george stanley.' [See also Christ Church MS. 183, fol. 9^a.]
fol. 81^b.	More scribbles of verses in various hands. One quatrain is in Salusbury's hand :

> He plowes the skyes and fishes for the winde
> and sowes his seede vppon the barren sande
> that puttes great trust or seekes good happ to fynd
> In any fickel waveringe woemans hand.
> J. S.

In the hand which wrote XXVI, XXVIII, and XXIX:

> Whose brused barke the wawes in twayen doo tosse
> delytes no more in surge of sees to daunsse
> And he that once hath suffred shypwrackes losse
> doth learne at laste to shonne the licke myschaunce
> the fishe that feles and scapes the flatering bayte
> will all wayes feare to fynd the lycke decete.

Other rhyming lines (in different hands) are the following:

> Faith woemens love is but an appetite
> or att the best, but humor or a passion
> the [they?] weare affection as the weare a fashion.
>   J. S.

> Our love from an imperious bouldnes nere can sunder
> We love them most y^t most will keepe vs vnder.
>   S. V.

> Though thus I yield lett nott your passion waste
> She y^{tes} most coy is ever fownd most chaste.
>   H. H.

fol 82–83ᵃ.   Verses by Danielle; text printed—Nos. XXI and XXII. Along the side margins of fol. 82ᵃ are two quatrains in different hands:

> most woemen suer ar feeckel and vnkynd
> thear thoughtes doth vary oftener then the wind
> but yeat sum ar most constant & most true
> but thoes be Rare, my fayth assuereth you
>   finis J. A. (?)

> good god be allwayes my defence
> and sylde me from all yll,
> defende mee from my enimies
> And from ther Raginge will.
>   finis J. S.

fol. 83ᵇ.   Verses by Hughe Gryphyth; text printed—No. XXIII. These verses are written on a sheet of smaller size which has been pasted upon this page in the book. Below the English lines is a quatrain in Welsh, in another hand.

Introduction xxxv

fol. 84. Verses headed 'J. S. his amasement'; text printed—No. XXIV. This leaf, of different size and paper from the others, has been bound into the book at this point.

fol. 86ᵇ. Latin acrostic verses; text printed—No. XXV. At the foot of the page, four lines in Welsh with the signature, 'Llewys Dwnn, 1596.'

fol. 87ᵃ. An acrostic poem; text printed—No. XXVI.

fol. 87ᵇ. 'Poysies' on the occasion of Salusbury's marriage; text printed—No. XXVII.

fol. 88. Two acrostic poems in the same hand as No. XXVI; text printed—Nos. XXVIII and XXIX.

fol. 89–174 are in the hand of William Kynwal and consist entirely of Welsh poems, by a number of poets, in praise of the ancestors of Catherine of Berain and her first and second husbands, Mr. John Salusbury and Sir Richard Clough. The last in the series is a poem by Kynwal in praise of Catherine of Berain herself.

fol. 174–199ᵇ contain a series of fourteen elegies upon Catherine of Berain, the first three in Latin, the next three in English, and the rest in Welsh. See Nos. XXX–XXXV.

On the lower portion of fol. 178ᵇ is the following entry in Sir John Salusbury's hand:

Jane	God toock to his mercy the sole
Theloall	of my deare syster Jane wynn wife
deceased	to Mʳ Symon Theloall Sunday
the 11th daye	beinge the eleuenth daye of maye
of maye 1606.	in the yeare of our lorde god 1606.

fol. 200–300 contain a long list of Welsh poems, addressed to various members of the Salusbury family;

also several addressed to Jesus Christ. The earlier poems in this series are composed in praise of Mr. John Salusbury, the first husband of Catherine of Berain. On fol. 267 and fol. 276 are two poems in honour of Ursula, the wife of Sir John Salusbury. The latter piece is signed by 'Edward bryn llys'.

fol. 300^b (a fly-leaf) contains two distiches in the hand of Sir John Salusbury:

> who labores that to bringe to passe
> that cannot be is but an asse.
>
> wth sum light thinge when thow needes most
> trie thy frend before thow trust.

From this list of the contents of the two Salusbury MSS. it will be seen that the material directly relating to our present inquiry is confined to MS. 184. The original portion of this volume was written by the well-known bard, William Kynwal of Penmachno.[1] In his preface he states that he began his task, at the request of Catherine of Berain, in the year 1570. Since it contains no mention of Morris Wynn we may conclude that Kynwal's compilation was completed before Catherine's marriage to her third husband. Kynwal has embellished his portion of the manuscript by heading the several poems with coloured drawings of the family arms—either the white lion of the Salusbury or the Saracen's head of Catherine's house. After the death of Catherine of Berain in 1591 the volume was continued by adding a series of elegies celebrating her memory, as well as several poems in honour of her first husband—John Salusbury, Esq., father of our Sir John Salusbury—and also a number of miscellaneous compositions.

Finally, between the pedigree of Catherine and the first of the series of poems commemorating her ancestors (fol. 89)

---

[1] Kynwal died in 1587; cf. *Hist. MSS. Com.*, Report on Welsh MSS., i. 1034.

A Conceite

47

Ston afford it feele heate euery howr
And is a poyson hot and sharp
And by expedience is so knowne
&c &c matter &c by some
And last doth grow of sundry seedes
At last do proue but stinking weedes
And if quick weede be found in feild
Of the wheate deuision it makes

Finis John Salusbury

A Conceite to the former

A base bread hagyard that by chaunce doth light
vpon the Imperious eagle in her flight
and gainst all nature in her nest doth breed
and with her eagles food his yong ones feed
had this great grace albeit he basards minde,
yet must be for kitt will after y[e] kind:
hauinge no name but given by the my[gh]t
in basenes borne and no by basenes rought
for hauinge stole a name from gentry
crost is his coate by careful heraldrie:
base gantlie giuen did for his kindred blott
that in this fortune he himselfe forgott:
But Ioues great bird doth laugh this kyte to scorne
as if his kinred his basenes had outworne
and since his winges he had not mount so high
but fall into the case of beggary

Finis

one finds a quantity of miscellaneous material, prose and verse, written in both English and Welsh. Of these leaves, fols. 34–41 and 82–84 were originally loose sheets which have since been collected and bound into the volume in their present position. This portion of the manuscript, indeed, seems to be a family scrap-book into which were gathered pieces of verse, recipes, memoranda and idle scribblings. The fact that nearly everything in this miscellany is directly connected in some way with Sir John Salusbury, and that the latest date which appears is 1606 (in the entry in which Sir John records the death of his sister) would indicate that this material was inserted in the volume during Sir John's life, probably under his personal supervision.

These leaves have been written by a number of hands, most of which cannot be identified. The verses by Ben Jonson (see below, No. III)—originally written upon a loose sheet—are in the poet's own hand. The subscription, 'finis quoth Danielle,' at the end of Nos. XXI and XXII has been added by another hand. Neither the hand of the text nor that of the signatures appears elsewhere in the MS. The 'Danielle' of these pieces may possibly be Samuel Daniel, but on the whole this appears to me altogether unlikely.[1]

Though Salusbury's characteristic signature (see frontispiece), or at least his initials, are appended to a number of poems, in most cases it would seem that the text itself was written by another hand—as is the case with his letter to Cecil reproduced above. The clearest example of a poem written by Salusbury's own hand is No. XV, on the lower half of fol. 47, of which a rotographic reproduction is presented herewith.

The hand which appears most frequently in these leaves

---

[1] These pieces were written after the death of Vrsula Salusbury's father, the fourth Earl of Derby (see below, No. XXII, lines 9–10), which occurred in 1593. His son Ferdinando, the fifth Earl, died in 1594 and was succeeded by his brother William. It is not certain which brother is the one referred to by Danielle.

is Robert Chester's. All the poems to which Chester's name is attached, with the single exception of the Blanch Wynn acrostic (No. VI), are written and signed by his own hand. In addition to these, Nos. IV, VII, XIV, and XVIII appear to be in his hand, as well as fol. 49^b, containing the memorandum of fees paid at the knighting of Salusbury. Chester writes not only the familiar national hand most frequently used by Elizabethan scribes, but also the Italian hand. Sometimes (as in Nos. VII and XVII) he begins a piece in the Italian and completes it in the national script. Again, in No. X, which is written in the national script, he employs the Italian hand for the flower-names—both on the margin and in the text. A specimen of Chester's national hand may be seen in the short poem at the top of fol. 47^a (reproduced above in facsimile).

No less than nine of the poems here printed from Christ Church MS. 184 contain acrostics. In Nos. V and VI we find the name of Blanch Wynn, who (as noted below) was the wife of Edward Wynn, Sir John Salusbury's half-brother. In No. XXV (a Latin poem in praise of Sir John) the acrostic letters spell IOHANNES SALVSBVRIVS. But far the most frequent are the DOROTHY HALSALL acrostics. Her name appears alone in Nos. VIII, IX, XXVI, XXVIII, and XXIX, and in No. X it occurs joined with IOHN SALVSBVRY in an ingenious double acrostic.[1] Moreover, in the lyrics addressed to her a warmth of passion appears which suggests that Sir John found her a thoroughly fascinating person.

Dorothy was a natural daughter of Henry Stanley, fourth Earl of Derby, by Jane Halsall of Knowsley,[2] and was accordingly a sister-in-law of Sir John Salusbury. She married Cuthbert Halsall, Esq., of Halsall and Clifton, Lancashire, by whom she had two daughters : Ann, who became

---

[1] A somewhat similar use of the double acrostic is to be noted in one of the poems by Humphrey Gifford (1580), edited by Dr. Grosart, *Miscellanies of The Fuller Worthies' Library*, i. 315-17.

[2] *Victorian Co. Hist. of Lancashire*, as cited above, p. xv, note 4.

Introduction xxxix

the wife of Thomas Clifton, Esq., of Westby, and Bridget, who married Thomas Crompton, Esq.[1] Cuthbert Halsall was Justice of the Peace in 1595,[2] an office which he held for a number of years. He was knighted at Dublin, July 22, 1599, being apparently in the suite of the Earl of Essex,[3] and in 1601 he was High Sheriff of Lancashire.[4] In 1605 he was a recusant, and the profits of his forfeitures as such were assigned to Sir Thomas Mounson.[5] In Jan. 1624-5, we find record of an effort to restore to him his ancient inheritance,[6] but it is doubtful whether the attempt succeeded, for in 1628 he was again certified as a recusant.[7]

I find no record of the year of his death, but it is clear that his wife survived him, for in 1632 and 1633 'Dame Dorothy' appears in certain legal documents as his widow and executrix.[8]

From these facts in the life of Sir Cuthbert Halsall, however, we get no information concerning the relations of Dorothy Halsall and Sir John Salusbury. The Halsall acrostics printed in the Parry volume show that Sir John's infatuation for his sister-in-law began before 1597, but we have no means of knowing how long it continued. Several allusions in the poems addressed to her make it clear that she was already married. In view of Sir John's unfriendliness toward the followers of Essex it is a bit odd to find that Dorothy's husband was of the Essex party and a recusant as well.

For our present purpose the most important contribution

[1] Josiah Rose, *Lancashire and Cheshire Histor. and Genealog. Notes*, i. (1879), 261.
[2] *Hist. MSS. Com.*, Report xiv, App., part iv, 583.
[3] Metcalfe, *Book of Knights*, p. 209.
[4] *Acts of the Privy Council*, 1600–1, p. 256.
[5] *Victorian Co. Hist. of Lancashire*, iii. 195.
[6] *Hist. MSS. Com.*, Report xii, App., part i, 181.
[7] *Hist. MSS. Com.*, Report xiii, App., part i, 1.
[8] *Victorian Co. Hist. of Lancashire*, iii. 196, footnote; also *Calendar of Lancash. and Cheshire Exchequer Depositions by Commission*, ed. Caroline Fishwick, Lanc. and Chesh. Record Soc., xi (1885), p. 24.

made by this collection of poems in the Christ Church MS. consists in the new light which they throw upon the relations between Sir John Salusbury and Robert Chester. The discussion of these Chester poems and their bearing upon the problem of *Loves Martyr* may, however, be taken up more conveniently after we have considered the series of poems by Salusbury preserved in the Parry volume.

III. THE SALUSBURY POEMS IN THE PARRY VOLUME

The other collection of Salusbury poems, which is presented in the following pages, is included in a small 12mo volume of verse, which bears upon the title-page the name 'Robert Parry, Gent.' Parry was himself of Denbighshire, and owed friendly allegiance to the house of Lleweni.[1] It will be remembered that he contributed an elegy on the death of Sir John's mother, Catherine of Berain.[2] Of his personal history we know but little, though our information will be materially increased by the publication of his Diary.[3] Parry seems to have travelled somewhat widely: he made repeated visits to London,[4] and in 1600 he made a six-months' journey to Italy. His friends spoke of him respectfully as a man of learning. In 1595 Parry published a prose novel —interspersed after the fashion of the day with numerous lyrics[5]—to which he gave the title, *Moderatus, the most delectable and famous Historie of the Black Knight*, and which

[1] It may be noted that Robert Parry's brother, Richard, married Blanche, daughter of Edward Thelwall, Sir John Salusbury's stepfather; and that their son, John Parry, married Oriana Salusbury, daughter of Sir John.

[2] Christ Church MS. 184, fol. 179; see below, p. 41.

[3] The MS. of Parry's Diary is in the possession of Col. T. A. Wynne Edwards of Plâs Nantglyn. An edition of it is being prepared by A. Foulkes-Roberts, Esq., of Denbigh.

[4] In his Diary he speaks of witnessing the Queen's procession in state to St. Paul's, Nov. 24, 1588, 'beinge within on moneth after my comynge to London the second tyme.' Again he mentions being at the Court at Windsor in the 35th year of Elizabeth.

[5] The first of these has been reprinted in *Censura Literaria*, x, 311.

Introduction xli

he dedicated, 'To the right Worshipfull / And his singvlar good Master, / Henry Townshend, Esquire, one of her Maiesties Iustices of / Assise of the countie Pallatine of Chester, and one of / her Highnesse honourable Counsell, established / in the marches and principality of Wales.'

Two years later appeared the little book of poems with which we are at present concerned. The only surviving copy of this book is now in the library of S. R. Christie-Miller, Esq., at Britwell Court. The title-page is as follows:

> SINETES
> Passions vppon his fortunes,
> offered for an Incense at the
> shrine of the Ladies which gui-
> ded his distempered
> thoughtes.
> The Patrons patheticall Po-
> sies, Sonets, Maddrigals, and
> Roundelayes. Together with
> Sinetes Dompe.
> Plena verecundi culpa pudoris erat.
> By ROBERT PARRY.
> Gent.
> At LONDON.
> Printed by T. P. for William
> Holme, and are to be sould on
> Ludgate hill at the signe of
> the holy Lambe.
> 1597.

The first three pages (Sig. A 2–A 3 recto) contain Parry's poem dedicating the volume—

> To the right worshipfull John
> Salisburye of Lleweni Esquier
> for the Bodie to the Queenes
> most excellent Maiestie.

These verses (ten 6-line stanzas) have been reprinted by Dr. Grosart.[1] Next comes a series of brief commendatory poems signed as below:

Sig. A 3 verso 'Vppon the Authors muse,' signed, 'Hu. Gry.'

[1] Introduction to Chester's *Loves Martyr*, pp. xiv–xv.

Sig. A 4 verso 'In prayse of the Booke,' signed, 'H. P. gentleman.'

Sig. A 5 recto 'In prayse of the Booke,' signed, 'W. R. Gent.'

Sig. A 5 verso 'In prayse of the Booke,' signed, 'H. P. Gent.'

Sig. A 6 recto 'In prayse of the Booke,' signed, 'T. S. Esq.'

Sig. A 6 verso 'In prayse of the Booke,' signed, 'R. S. Esq.'

Sig. A 7 recto 'In prayse of the Booke,' signed, 'W. M. Esq.'

The 'Passions', which form the main division of the book, begin on the following page (Sig. A 7 verso). They are forty-six in number, each occupying a single page. An examination of these 'Passions' discloses the curious fact that they are arranged so as to form acrostics. Reading their initial letters, one finds that they spell three names: FRANSIS WYLOWGHBY, ELYZABETH WOLFRESTON, ROBERT PARRY. The appearance of these names might at first suggest that the 'Passions' were the result of collaboration by these three persons. Against such a supposition, however, is the statement on the title-page: 'Sinetes Passions vppon *his* fortunes.' The meaning of 'Sinetes' is a puzzle, but it plainly stands for one person and not three. The title-page informs us further that the author offers these Passions 'for an Incense at the shrine of the Ladies which guided his distempered thoughts'. What is more natural, then, than that Parry should couple with his own name in the acrostics the names of these ladies? Accordingly, we may safely conclude that the ladies who inspired these Passions were Frances Willoughby[1] and Elizabeth Wolfreston.

The former, by an extremely plausible conjecture, may be

---

[1] The discrepancy between 'Fransis' and 'Frances' will trouble no one who is familiar with the vagaries of Elizabethan spelling.

identified as Frances, the sixth and youngest daughter of Sir Francis Willoughby of Wollaton Hall, Notts. The early life of Frances Willoughby was made most unhappy by the harsh and unnatural treatment which she and her sisters received from her mother.[1] Finding life at home insupportable, Frances, who was a high-spirited girl, at length ran away in company with Mr. John Drake, who took her to the home of his uncle Richard Drake. To her father, for whom she still cherished sincere affection, she dispatched a letter explaining her action. In this letter she declared, 'that her mother's cruelty to her had forced her to take this course, and tho' she was sensible she ought not to accuse her mother, yet now such was her offence that only her mother's wrongs could render her excusable and his knowing that she never used to displease him. She writ that Mr. Drake used her with great respect and took care to preserve her reputation and that her intention was to live for some time in his uncle Richard Drake's house, whose wife had an extraordinary good character, and there she hoped to carry herself so well as to merit his pleasure.'[2] The date of Frances Willoughby's departure from home is not recorded, but it must have been before 1594, the year of her mother's death, and it probably was within two or three years of that date. She remained under the protection of the Drakes for several years and probably until her marriage to Montague Wood of Lambley, Notts, an event which occurred before May, 1600.[3]

[1] Our chief source of information concerning the Willoughby family is the Collections made in 1702 by Cassandra Willoughby, who had access to many letters and private papers which are no longer extant. These have been printed with some abridgements by the *Hist. MSS. Com.* in the Report on the MSS. at Wollaton Hall (1911).

[2] Quoted from Cassandra Willoughby's Collections, *Hist. MSS. Com.*, Report on MSS. at Wollaton Hall, p. 607.

[3] As shown by a letter from Wood to Abigail Willoughby, Frances's sister, dated May 14, 1600 (*ibid.*, p. 170). In this letter Wood makes a scandalous report of his wife's behaviour, but his testimony is discounted to some extent by the ill character given him by Cassandra Willoughby, who speaks in strong terms of his cruel treatment of his wife (*loc. cit. supra*).

It must be confessed that we lack any positive evidence of Robert Parry's acquaintance with the runaway daughter of Sir Francis Willoughby. At the same time the dates, the circumstances, and the character of the young lady make this identification in every way an attractive conjecture. Concerning Elizabeth Wolfreston, the other lady whom Parry names, I can find no information. Wolfreston is the name of a family which was connected a little later with the Manor of Preese, Amounderness Hundred, Lancashire.[1] Again, there was a Capt. Wolverstone who served in Ireland in the Essex campaign.[2] But it should also be noted that according to the Visitations of the Co. of Nottingham in Harl. MS. 1400, Wollaton, the seat of Sir Francis Willoughby, is spelled 'Wolverton'.

This digression in pursuit of the ladies named in Robert Parry's acrostics would hardly have been pertinent to our present inquiry were it not for the fact that the acrostics, FRANCIS WILOWBI, ELIZABETH WOLFRESTONE, and ROBERT PARRYE meet us again in a poem which will be discussed presently, and with them in this case are joined DOROTHI HALSALL and IOHN SALESBVRYE. The association of these names in the same poem suggests at least that Salusbury, too, may have enjoyed acquaintance with the ladies who inspired Parry's 'Passions'.

We are ready at length to examine 'the Patrone's' portion of Robert Parry's volume, which immediately follows the 'Passions', headed by a separate title-page (see below, p. 46). Dr. Grosart noted the occurrence of these poems, clearly marked off in this manner from the other contents of the volume, and he remarks concerning them: 'it is just barely possible (though I confess improbable) that Sir John Salisburie is their author' (p. xvii). Had he recognized the acrostics which they contain his joy would have been full, for these

[1] See MS. of the House of Lords, *Hist. MSS. Com.*, Report iii, App., p. 30ᵃ.
[2] *Hist. MSS. Com.*, Report on MSS. at Hatfield House, part ix, 146, 330

supply positive proof of Salusbury's authorship. A more remarkable series of acrostic verses never existed outside the dreams of the most ardent Baconian. In reprinting these poems herewith I have displayed the acrostic letters in bold-face type lest some of them should elude the reader's eye—indeed I am not certain that I have caught all of them myself. Posie I presents us again with the name DOROTHY HALSAL—already thoroughly familiar to us through the Christ Church MS. In Posie II we have the same name spelled backwards. In Posie III we find (also in reverse order) the three names: DOROTHY CVTBERT halsall—the last being formed of the terminal letters immediately preceding the caesura.[1] The three names are explained when one remembers that Sir John's sister-in-law married Cuthbert Halsall. Finally, it is to be noted that the first and last words in the last line of this Posie give us Salusbury's initials: 'I. S.'

Posie IIII is easily the most complicated in the series, and requires more detailed examination. In the first place the title, 'The Patrons pauze in ode,' suggests that this piece interrupts the series of Salusbury poems. In my opinion when the Patron paused Robert Parry resumed. For note that the last lines of the stanzas, which together spell IOHN SALESBVRYE, may be read independently of their context as seven short couplets, and that when thus read they appear to be *addressed to* Salusbury and not written by him. In particular, 'Hope of our time,' at the end of stanza 3 reads like an echo of the first line of Parry's dedicatory poem, in which Salusbury is addressed as—

   The Hope of these, and glasse of future times.

Proceeding with the acrostics in Posie IIII, one perceives that the first lines of the stanzas spell DOROTHI HALSALL, while the second lines give us FRANSIS WILOWBI. But the resources of the acrostic poet are not yet exhausted. If the initial

   It was the vigilant eye of Professor W. A. Neilson which first detected the 'halsall', after these poems were already in type.

letters of the four lines which remain in each stanza are read in order as they come we get in the first eight stanzas : ELIZ-ABET-HWOL-FRES-TONE-ROBE-RTPA-RRYE. At this point, unfortunately, material ran short, and consequently the remaining six stanzas lack this portion of the elaborate acrostic system. The recurrence of the names of Frances Willoughby, Elizabeth Wolfreston, and Robert Parry in this poem confirms me in my opinion that Posie IIII is not the work of the Patron.

Posie V contains no acrostics ; nevertheless one suspects that under the word-play a personal allusion may be concealed. Though this piece affords no decisive evidence of authorship I am inclined to believe that it is Salusbury's and not Parry's. In any case there can be no question about Posie 6, which bears the title, 'The patrones Dilemma,' and contains the acrostic, DOROTHY HALSALL.

Posie VIII likewise contains a Dorothy Halsall acrostic, together with the initials 'I. S.' in the concluding line. The heading which it bears—'The Patrones Adiew'—may possibly suggest that it is Salusbury's final contribution to the series of 'Posies'—as it certainly is the last which contains acrostics.

The thirteen 'Posies' are followed by a series of thirty-one 'Sonettos', of which only six contain acrostics. The line initials of Sonetto 3 give us 'I. S. HIS VALENTINE' —a sufficient assurance of Salusbury's authorship—and Sonettos 4 and 5 contain (with slightly varied spelling) the name ELEANOR SALVSBVRY—a person whom I have not succeeded in identifying. The other three acrostic Sonettos— 16, 17, and 18—when read from the bottom yield the name, HELENA OWEN—who likewise is a person unknown. I see no reason why the entire series of Sonettos, as well as the Madrigals and Roundelays which follow, should not be assigned to Salusbury, especially as 'Sonets, Maddrigalls, & Rowndelayes' are specifically mentioned in the title-page prefixed to the Patron's division of the book.

This (so far as the evidence goes) completes Salusbury's

share in the volume—a total of exactly fifty pages, if we deduct Posie IIII and assign him all the others. 'Sinetes Dumpe,' which follows, is, of course, the work of Parry. Who the Nameless Malcontent may be, with whose Lamentation the volume concludes, we have no means of determining. In tone as well as theme it resembles much of Salusbury's verse and it is possible that it comes from his pen—but there are no acrostics to betray the secret.

IV. Who was Robert Chester?

We come finally to inquire in regard to Robert Chester and the relationship in which he stood to Sir John Salusbury. At the very outset we are confronted by the problem of the poet's identity. The only attempt thus far to solve this problem is that which has been made by Dr. Grosart, who has gone to much pains to identify the author of *Loves Martyr* with Robert Chester, Esq., of Royston, Herts., though he was not able to establish any connexion between this Hertfordshire squire and Sir John Salusbury, to whom *Loves Martyr* was dedicated, or to discover in Chester of Royston the slightest tendency toward poetry or literature of any sort. Before discussing this attempt to identify Robert Chester the poet, it is necessary to consider briefly such biographical evidence as is obtainable concerning the Royston claimant. So far as the family history of the Royston Chesters is concerned, little need be added to the material presented by Dr. Grosart (pp. vii–viii). Edward Chester, the father of Robert, served in the Low Countries under the Prince of Orange, who rewarded him for his sturdy defence of Delft in 1573 by advancing him from the rank of captain to that of colonel. A further testimony to his military services appears in the grant by the States of Holland, under date September 19, 1581, of an annual pension of twenty-four guilders, to be paid to him as long as he should live, and afterwards to be continued to his son Robert for the term of his life.[1]

Robert Chester of Royston was born, as Dr. Grosart has shown, about the end of June, 1566. It is possible that he was a University man, for there is record of a Robert Chester who proceeded B.A. from Trinity College, Cambridge, in 1585-6.[2] On July 30, 1587, Robert Chester of Royston was married to Anne, daughter of Sir Henry Capell, of Little Hadham, Herts.[3] Of this union were born four sons and five daughters.[4] During the whole time from his marriage until 1600 Robert Chester appears to have been closely connected with local affairs in Hertfordshire. In 1593 his name stands in a list of gentlemen of this county who were assessed on a 'contribution' for the defence of the kingdom. The assessments range from £20 to £50, Chester's being £30.[5] May 22, 1597, Robert Chester and four others were appointed to receive, disburse, and account to the deputy lieutenants for, all moneys issued and levied in the several Hundreds in the County toward fitting out troops for the wars.[6] Two

---

[1] See Sir Roger Williams's account of the campaigns in the Low Countries (*Somers' Tracts*, i. 374). For the date and terms of the pension granted to Edward Chester, see Lansdowne MS. 145, fol. 80, which is a copy ('Translated out of Duche') of an Act by the States of Holland, October 31, 1587, in which the terms of the original grant are rehearsed. In Robert Chester's will, dated May 3, 1638 (Prerogative Court of Canterbury, '25 Evelyn,' preserved at Somerset House), mention is made of 'my pencion from the states of Holland and the arrearages thereof'.

[2] I am under obligations to Mr. J. A. Venn for this information. Unfortunately, since the admission books of this college do not begin until later, we lack any record of the age or birthplace of this Robert Chester, B.A., and therefore have no means of identifying him. Of the two Universities it is much more probable that Chester of Royston would have gone up to Cambridge, which is only a few miles distant from his home.

[3] Duncan Warrand, *Hertfordshire Families*, 1907, p. 89.

[4] I follow the list given in Mundy's Visitation of Hertfordshire, 1634 (Harl. MS. 1547, fol. 13b, Harleian Soc. Pubs., xxii, p. 40), which appears to be more authentic than that given in Mundy's Visitation of 1620 (Harl. MS. 1546, fol. 75b). According to the latter there were five sons and six daughters.

[5] Cussan, *Hist. of Hertfordshire*, Hundred of Edwinstree, p. 7.

[6] *Calendars of State Papers, Domestic*, 1596-7, p. 417.

Introduction

years later Chester was a Justice of the Peace and also held the office of High Sheriff for the County of Herts. A further bit of evidence showing Chester's close touch with local affairs appears in a letter from Sir Arthur Capell to Cecil, May 2, 1600. Sir Arthur states that he has been entreated by his brother-in-law, Mr. Robert Chester, to inform Cecil of his knowledge concerning the insufficiency of the townsmen of Royston to undergo so great a charge as the building up of their church.[1] Moreover, between 1596 and 1600 Robert Chester was actively engaged in business transactions, buying and selling a number of pieces of property, chiefly in Hertfordshire.[2] Down to the year 1600, then, the circumstances in the life of Robert Chester of Royston, so far as we know them, afforded no opportunity for association with John Salusbury, of Lleweni. In that year for the first time we find a possible link which would serve to connect the two men. On February 14, 1600, Robert Chester of Royston, Esq., was admitted to the Middle Temple,[3] to which Salusbury had been admitted some five years earlier. Apparently Chester retained his chamber at the Middle Temple until the autumn of 1601.[4] The coincidence of Chester's residence at the Temple with the publication of *Loves Martyr* would have

---

[1] *Hist. MSS. Com.*, Report on MSS. at Hatfield House, part x, 135.

[2] Patent Rolls, Public Record Office: Sept. 2, 1596 (38 Eliz., Pars viii), Mar. 2, 1598 (40 Eliz., iv), Oct. 20, 1599 (41 Eliz., xxii). See also deeds preserved at the Brit. Mus.: Sept. 27, 1597 (Add. Chart. 36264); Nov. 9, 1598, June 26, 1599, Oct. 22, 1599, Nov. 24, 1599 (Add. Charts. 36266–9).

[3] The record of his admission reads as follows: ' 14 Feb. [1600, New Style] Robert Chester of Royston, Herts, esq., specially; fine, only 20 s., at the instance of Mr. Shurley, a Master of the Bench. Bound with Messrs. George Shurley and Frances Clyve. Also to the chamber of Messrs. George Shurley and Henry Tokefeilde, esq., in place of the latter; fine only 20 s., at the instance of Mr. Shurley of the Bench ' (Hopwood, *Middle Temple Records*, i. 402). I confess that I do not understand this last sentence. Possibly two admission entries have been 'telescoped'.

[4] The date of his withdrawal is fixed approximately by the following entry in the Middle Temple Records (ed. Hopwood, p. 417): ' 27 Nov. [1601] Mr. William Pemberton to the chamber of Messrs. George Shurley and Robert Chester in place of the latter; fine, 30 s.'

given much satisfaction to Dr. Grosart had he known of it. And if we had to take into account merely the dedication of *Loves Martyr* to Salusbury, there is no doubt that the Middle Temple connexion might be accepted as evidence in favour of the identification of Robert Chester of Royston as the poet. But it is now necessary to consider also the Chester poems in the Christ Church MS.; and these make it clear that the friendship between the poet and Salusbury began at least two years before 1600. Accordingly the Middle Temple will not serve as the means of introducing them to each other. Furthermore, so far as Chester of Royston is concerned, his residence at the Middle Temple seems to have been brought about not by Salusbury, but by George Shirley,[1] with whom he was associated in a series of business transactions, including several of the purchases of property to which reference has been made above.

These biographical data concerning Robert Chester of Royston, we must conclude, offer no support to the identification which Dr. Grosart has proposed. His unbroken connexion with Hertfordshire down to 1600 is not easily reconciled with Robert Chester the poet, who offered his 'Wynter Garland of Sommer Flowers' (No. X) to Salusbury as a New Year's gift in 1598. For it is to be observed that Chester the poet writes from the point of view of Denbighshire. He composes verses of welcome when Sir John Salusbury comes down from the Court to Lleweni,[2] or again he

---

[1] The Shirley family, Mr. C. E. A. Bedwell, Librarian of the Middle Temple, informs me, was closely associated with the Capell family into which Robert Chester of Royston married. According to a pedigree of the Capell family printed by the Harleian Society (vol. xxii, p. 114), Frances Capell, the sister of Anne, wife of Robert Chester, married a Shirley—very probably George Shirley. George Shirley himself was a Middle Templer of influence. He had been called to the degree of 'le Utter Barr' in 1597 (Hopwood, i. 374), and later became Reader and at length Master of the Bench.

[2] Cf. No. XVII (p. 25). Note especially the lines:

> Then how I joy at theese weekes happie ending,
> Let my forepassed greef at full relate,
> How pleasure in my brest the time is spending
> That whilome liude Alone disconsolate.

I

Signature of Robert Chester the poet, Christ Church MS. 184, fol. 46ᵃ.

II

Signature of Robert Chester of Royston, B.M. Add. Chart. 36273.

III

Signature of the translator of De Optimo Senatore, B.M. Add. MS. 18613.

sings his patron's praise at a Christmas merriment held at Lleweni.[1] Note also that he appears to be thoroughly acquainted with the animosities in which Sir John was involved with some of his neighbours.[2] In a word, Chester the poet betrays a connexion with the region of Denbigh no less definite than the connexion of Chester of Royston with Hertfordshire. One feels, too, when the poet exhorts the swains of Arcady (i.e. Denbighshire) to

> sing a madringall or roundelay
> to please our Lordlike sheapheard lord of us,

that his attitude toward Salusbury resembles that of a feudal retainer rather than that which would be assumed by the Squire of Hertfordshire, who was himself of a prominent and established family.

Finally—if further evidence be needed—I place side by side on the opposite page facsimiles of the signatures of the two men. The first is the signature of Robert Chester the poet, at the end of his 'Wynter Garland of Sommer Flowers' (No. X), written in 1598. The second is the signature of Robert Chester of Royston, Esq., appended to a deed bearing date, May 1, 1602.

A Robert Chester, who assuredly is not the poet and possibly is to be distinguished also from the squire of Royston, appears as the author of an unprinted translation of the First Book of the treatise *De Optimo Senatore* by Laurentius Goslicius.[3] This piece of translation, preserved in B.M. Addit. MS. 18613, is evidently the work of a young student, probably either at the University or at one

[1] Cf. No. XII (p. 19).
[2] Cf. No. XIII (p. 20).
[3] Another translation of this treatise, printed at London in 1598 under the title: 'The Counsellor / Exactly pourtraited in two Bookes. / Wherein the Offices of / Magistrates, the happie life of Subiectes, and the felicitie of / Common-weales is pleasantly and pithilie discoursed,' &c., is wholly independent of Robert Chester's, and is distinctly a more careless piece of work.

of the Inns of Court. The dedicatory inscription (fol. 3ᵃ) reads:

> To the Right Worshipfull and his singular
> good freind Mr Meade Judge of the
> comon place Robert Chester wisheth
> long life, increase of hono*ur* with
> all prosperity.

In the Epistle to Judge Meade which follows, the translator gives some information about himself:

> I offer the first fruites of my labor and studyes vnto yow trusting that it shalbe as well accepted as though it had been more curious for the manner and copious for the matter. I hope yow will not looke that the plant newly graffed should bring forth fruit in such plentifull manner as the stock of longer graffe. . . . [fol. 3ᵇ] Well, when I shalbe better setled and of longer contynuance I hope I shall bring forth fruit both more toothsome for your taste, and more holesome for yo*ur* diet. In the meane tyme perswading nay assuring myself yᵗ this my paynes shalbe accepted in good part I cease to troble yow desrying th'almighty to protect yow and yo*ur* whole family from all perilles and preserue yow in all prosperity.

Thomas Meade, to whom this work was dedicated, came of an Essex family. He was elevated to the bench of the Court of Common Pleas November 30, 1577, and retained this office until his death in May, 1585.[1] Since these dates fix the limits within which the translation was composed, it will be seen that, if the translator was Robert Chester of Royston, he must have completed it before the end of his nineteenth year. The third facsimile facing the preceding page shows the signature of Robert Chester the translator. It bears as much resemblance, perhaps, to the signature of Chester of Royston as could be expected between the hand of the same person at the ages of 18 and 36.

Though we have not yet succeeded in discovering *who* Robert Chester was, the Christ Church MS. gives us much additional information concerning his relationship to his patron, Sir John Salusbury. His poems in this MS., as has already been noted, were clearly written in the neighbourhood

---

[1] Edw. Foss, *Judges of England*, Ed. 1857, v. 524.

of Lleweni, the seat of the Salusburys in Denbighshire.
The fact that he writes verses in praise of Blanch Wynn
(No. VI, p. 9), who married Sir John's half-brother, and
Dorothy Halsall (Nos. VIII and IX, pp. 13-14), Sir John's
sister-in-law, is evidence of familiar acquaintance with the
Salusbury family circle. Still more significant in this respect
is his poem linking together in acrostics the names of his
patron and Dorothy Halsall (No. X, pp. 15 ff.). Finally, the
memorandum, in Chester's hand (Christ Church MS. 184,
fol. 49^b), of the fees paid by Sir John Salusbury at the time
he was knighted, suggests that Chester may have been installed in the Salusbury household, possibly (if one might
guess) as family chaplain.[1] However this may be, he was
in any case a person of humble social station and his relation
toward his patron, though familiar, was always that of a
dependant. How else can we explain such lines as these
(No. X, p. 15):

> Therefore to thee sole patron of my good,
> I proffer vp the proffer of my hart,
> my vndeserved favoures vnderstood;
> to thee and none but thee I will impart:
> > O grace them with thy gratious gracing looke
> > that in pure kindnes much haue vndertooke.

The recognition that the friendship of Robert Chester
and Sir John Salusbury was not one of social equality but
that Chester was merely a satellite and dependant, helps us
to understand how the publication of *Loves Martyr* with its
appended ' Poeticall Essaies ' must have come about. Chester
himself would hardly have been able to secure contributions from Shakspere, Jonson, and the others, to grace his
volume. On the other hand, Salusbury, with the rank of
a Knight and with his position as Esquire of the body to
Elizabeth, would meet with no difficulty in soliciting these

---

[1] Following up this conjecture, I undertook to consult the records of the
diocese on the chance of finding mention of Chester's name, but I learned
that unluckily the Diocesan registry of St. Asaph had been destroyed
during the Commonwealth.

poems. The presence in the Salusbury MS. at Christ Church of a poem written by Jonson's own hand makes one surmise that with him, at least, Sir John Salusbury had more than mere acquaintance. Also the lines with which Robert Chester begins his 'Welcome Home' to his patron, carry an interesting suggestion that Salusbury enjoyed personal association with the greater Elizabethans :

> Your eares hauing hard the Nightingall soe long,
> I feare will blame my hoarse-throat rauens song :
> The swanns that laue their blacke feet in the streames,
> Haue in their sweetnes sang you golden theames :
> Court-bewtefying Poets in their verse,
> Homerian like sweete stanzoes did rehearse. ·

One may most easily account for the publication of *Loves Martyr*, then, by supposing that Sir John Salusbury, in order to gratify the literary ambition of Chester, who was his friend as well as his dependant, took the MS. of the poem with him on one of his journeys from Lleweni to London, asked a few of the most prominent poets—'the best and chiefest of our moderne writers', as they are styled on the title-page—to lend their names and verses to the success of the volume, and then sent it to the printer. If such was indeed the case, Robert Chester must have been filled with true prophetic afflatus when he wrote of his patron three years before :

> Goodmeaning tells me he my freind will stand,
> To vnderprop my tottering rotten ryme !

V. THE ALLEGORY IN 'LOVES MARTYR'

Robert Chester's *Loves Martyr or Rosalins Complaint*, as it is styled on the title-page, falls easily into three general divisions : (1) The Allegory of the Turtle and Phoenix, which consists for the most part of a dialogue between the Phoenix and her instructor, Dame Nature ; (2) 'The Birth, Life, and Death of honourable Arthur King of Brittaine,' a narrative composed on the basis of the Elizabethan Chronicle Histories ; (3) a series of ' Cantoes ' (i.e. lyrics) addressed to the Phoenix by the ' Paphian Doue '.

Introduction

Of these three divisions the one dealing with King Arthur is thrust in extraordinary fashion into the very midst of the Dialogue between Dame Nature and the Phoenix. 'Here endeth', the poet remarks at its conclusion, 'the Birth, Life, Death, and Pedigree of King Arthur of Brittanie, & now, to where we left.' It is clear that this awkward interruption of the allegory was not a part of Chester's original plan but was an afterthought, suggested, as he explains in his preliminary remarks 'To the courteous Reader', by Dame Nature's reference to Arviragus and Arthur in connexion with the account of Windsor Castle. The King Arthur section, accordingly, may be regarded as a later insertion in the poem. As it lacks all connexion with the allegory of the Phoenix and Turtle, it may here be dismissed from further consideration.

In the 'Cantoes' which form the third division of *Loves Martyr* the allegory of the Phoenix and Turtle is continued. In these pieces, however, the Turtle-dove is himself the speaker and addresses the Phoenix in terms of ardent passion. These lyrics are arranged under two headings: (1) 'Cantoes Alphabet-wise to faire Phœnix made by the Paphian Doue;' (2) 'Cantoes Verbally Written,' in which the first words of each line form rhyming sentences. In constructing these 'verbally written' stanzas Chester has borrowed liberally from current 'ring posies', as is evident from the following parallels which appear in a collection of these 'posies' preserved in Harl. MS. 6910 (the page references are to Bullen, *Some Shorter Elizabethan Poems*):

'LOVES MARTYR.'	HARL. MS.
Myselfe and mine, are always thine (p. 145).	Myself and mine are only thine (p. 274, col. 2).[1]
O let me heare, from thee my deare (p. 148).	I would I were With you, my Dear (p. 273, col. 1).
If I you haue, none else I craue (p. 149).	I nought do crave But you to have (p. 275, col. 2).

[1] Occurs also in Christ Church MS. 184, fol. 78^b.

'LOVES MARTYR.'	HARL. MS.
Be you to me, as I to thee (p. 149).	Be true to me, as I to thee (pp. 283 and 285).
If you I had, I should be glad (p. 150).	I would be glad If you I had (p. 273, col. 1).
I ioy to find a constant mind (p. 155).	I joy to find A constant mind (p. 274, col. 1).
Time shall tell thee, how well I loue thee (p. 165).	Time shall tell thee How much I love thee! (p. 274, col. 2).
The want of thee is death to me (p. 165).	The want of thee Is grief to me (p. 276, col. 2).
I loue to be beloued (p. 166).	Love to be loved (p. 274, col. 1).

There can be no doubt that the Phoenix and the Dove (or 'Turtle-Dove', pp. 152 and 158) of these Cantos are the same birds who figure in the earlier allegory. Compare, for example, the opening line of the 'Cantoes Alphabet-wise',

A Hill, a hill, a *Phœnix* seekes a Hill,

with the mention of the hill in 'Rosalins Complaint':

These shall direct him to this *Phœnix* bed,
Where on a high hill he this Bird shall meet.[1]

But the further question whether Robert Chester in these Cantos is uttering his own passion, as his employment of the first person would at first suggest, or was merely voicing the sentiments of the Turtle-dove, is one which can best be considered at a later point in the discussion.

With this glance at the several divisions into which *Loves Martyr* is separable we come at length to inquire as to the meaning of the allegory. And our present concern, it should be understood, is wholly with the Phoenix and Turtle of Chester's poem. The treatment of the allegory at the hands of Shakspere and the others who appended their 'poeticall essaies' will be postponed until the examination of Chester's allegory has been concluded. In embarking on this inquiry it will be convenient to have before us a brief synopsis of the story of the Phoenix and Turtle-dove as it stands in Chester's poem.

[1] *Loves Martyr*, p. 12.

Introduction lvii

Dame Nature finds the Phoenix in great dejection, lamenting that she 'must die And neuer [be] with a poore yong Turtle graced' (p. 16). Her beauty is unavailing since she is persecuted by Envy, and driven into exile by Fortune:

> What did my Beautie moue her to Disdaine ?
> Or did my Vertues shadow all her Blisse ?
> That she should place me in a desart Plaine,
> And send forth *Enuie* with a *Iudas* kisse,
> To sting me with a Scorpions poisoned hisse ?
>   From my first birth-right for to plant me heare,
>   Where I haue alwaies fed on Griefe and Feare (p. 23).

Nature banishes Envy, and promises better Fortune to the Phoenix (p. 23). She will bring her to the Ile of Paphos to visit the Turtle-dove. Accordingly they fly, 'Ouer the Semi-circle of *Europa*,' and come at length to England. During their flight Nature discourses of the history of various towns, which, however, are not introduced in any topographical order: (1) Athelney, (2) Winchester, (3) Oxford, (4) Leicester, (5) Canterbury, (6) Shaftsburie, (7) Carleyle, (8) Cambridge, (9) York, (10) Edinburgh, (11) Windsor, (12) London. At length they alight

> neere to that Ile
> In whose deep bottome plaines Delight doth smile (p. 81).

Then follows a long account of the plants, trees, fishes, gems, minerals, animals, and birds to be found in 'this louely Countrie'. Among the animals are the Camel and Elephant.

At the end of this long lecture by Dame Nature, the Phoenix spies the Turtle-dove—

> Whose feathers mowt off, falling as he goes,
> The perfect picture of hart pining woes (p. 123).

Nature explains who he is and discreetly withdraws:

> Farewell faire bird, Ile leaue you both alone,
> This is the *Doue* you long'd so much to see,
> And this will proue companion of your mone,
> An Vmpire of all true humility (p. 124).

In answer to the sympathetic inquiries of the Phoenix the Turtle replies:

> My teares are for my *Turtle* that is dead,
> My sorrow springs from her want that is gone,
> My heauy note sounds for the soule that's fled,
> And I will dye for him left all alone.[1]

Thereupon the Phoenix offers to share his grief:

> I will beare
> Halfe of the burdenous yoke thou dost sustaine.
> . . . .
> Thou shalt not be no more the *Turtle*-Doue,
> Thou shalt no more go weeping al alone,
> For thou shalt be my selfe, my perfect Loue,
> Thy griefe is mine, thy sorrow is my mone (pp. 126–7).

The Turtle is speedily consoled and both birds set to work light-heartedly to build the pyre upon which they propose to burn both their bodies 'to reuiue one name'. After prayers to Apollo they enter the flame—the Turtle first, then the Phoenix—and are consumed.

> 'And thus I end the *Turtle* Doues true story' (p. 131).

This line appears to bring the allegory to a natural conclusion; moreover, it is followed by 'Finis R. C.' It is quite possible, therefore, that the poem originally ended at this point and that the moralizing speech by the Pellican and the 'Conclusion' which follows it were added subsequently. It will be noted that with the beginning of the Pellican's speech the metre changes from stanzas to the couplet. Again, the final words of the Phoenix as she enters the flame—

> I hope of these another Creature springs,
> That shall possesse both our authority—

---

[1] The contradiction between 'her' in the second line and 'him' in the fourth line defies explanation. Mr. Herbert Collman assures me that this is the reading in the original print. Dr. Furnivall (p. 7* note) suggested the alteration of 'him' to 'her' in the fourth line. But it would be quite as easy to alter 'her' in the second line to 'his'. See below, p. lxiii.

should be compared with the definite announcement in the
'Conclusion':

> From the sweet fire of perfumed wood,
> Another princely *Phœnix* vpright stood:
> Whose feathers purified did yeeld more light,
> Then her late burned mother out of sight (p. 134).

Even this brief synopsis of Chester's allegory reveals its essentially grotesque character. And the conclusion leaves us uncertain whether to weep over the funeral pyre of the burned birds or to offer congratulations upon the birth of another Phoenix. In laying the scene for the poem Chester jumbles together Arabia, Paphos Isle, and Britain. There is the same bewildering confusion in the cyclopaedic catalogue of the fauna and flora of Paphos and its vicinity. Equally incongruous is the juxtaposition of the prayer to Jehovah (pp. 13-15) and the classical mythology of the scene with which the poem begins.

The confusions and obscurities which abound in Chester's poem result in part, no doubt, from careless and inartistic workmanship, but the radical defect lies in the unfortunate attempt to employ the allegory of the Phoenix as the basis of a poem to celebrate the union of two lovers. For if anything is clear in this poem, it is that the meeting of the Turtle and Phoenix is intended to represent a nuptial union. The Phoenix announces to the Turtle:

> we must wast together in that fire,
> That will not burne but by true Loues desire;

and again she bids him

> gather sweete wood for to make our flame,
> And in a manner sacrificingly,
> Burne both our bodies to reuiue one name.

A little later she declares:

> Of my bones must the Princely *Phœnix* rise;

and finally, addressing the fire, she cries:

> Accept into your euer hallowed flame,
> Two bodies, from the which may spring one name.

The Turtle, too, echoes this declaration :

> Accept my body as a Sacrifice
> Into your flame, of whom one name may rise.

The flame into which the Phoenix and Turtle plunged, then, was kindled by the torch of Hymen. This, no doubt, will explain the Turtle's reference to it as 'this happy Tragedy', and will enable us better to understand the fortitude of the Turtle as reported by the Pellican :

> With what a spirit did the *Turtle* flye
> Into the fire, and chearfully did dye ?
> He look't more pleasant in his countenance
> Within the flame, then when he did aduance,
> His pleasant wings vpon the naturall ground.

Nevertheless, one feels that in representing the nuptials of two happy lovers as an immolation—albeit a willing one—the poet has not chosen a fortunate figure, though it was the conclusion forced upon him by the allegory of the Phoenix.

This interpretation of the allegory may at first seem incompatible with certain lines in *Loves Martyr* which speak of the Turtle and the Phoenix as though they had actually perished in the flame. Perhaps the most explicit statement of this sort is one which occurs in the 'Conclusion' of the poem :

> From the sweet fire of perfumed wood,
> Another princely *Phœnix* vpright stood :
> Whose feathers purified did yeeld more light,
> Then her late burned mother out of sight (p. 134).

The last line apparently affirms unequivocally the death of the Phoenix, and hence would suggest that the catastrophe in the poem is to be understood as tragical. Nevertheless, this reference to the 'late burned mother' is to be regarded, I think, not as resting upon any basis of biographical fact, but as introduced merely for the sake of carrying out the Phoenix allegory. Indeed, these very lines afford an excellent illustration of the confusion into which Chester was led through the employment of an allegory which was ill suited to his purpose.

If we turn from the perplexing story of the Turtle-dove

and the Phoenix to 'The Authors request to the Phœnix', which immediately follows the Epistle Dedicatorie and is, as Dr. Grosart has observed, really a second dedication of the poem, we find the Phoenix not only surviving but standing forth as the patroness of the poet who has sung her incineration. The first stanza of the 'Authors request' runs as follows:

> Phœnix of beautie, beauteous Bird of any
> To thee I do entitle all my labour,
> More precious in mine eye by far then many,
> That feedst all earthly sences with thy sauour:
>   Accept my home-writ praises of thy loue,
>   And kind acceptance of thy *Turtle-doue*.

These lines are extremely important, not only because they make it clear that the story of the Phoenix and Turtle-dove is not to be regarded as ending tragically, but also because they afford assurance that a definite, personal interpretation underlies Chester's use of the allegory. For the poet would hardly have addressed this 'Request' to a mere abstraction. In the last two lines, moreover, we have a categorical statement of Chester's purpose in composing *Loves Martyr*. Accept my poem, he begs the Phoenix, which is written to celebrate your love and acceptance of the Turtle-dove.[1] The opinion expressed above that *Loves Martyr* was designed as a nuptial poem appears, therefore, to receive authoritative confirmation from Chester himself.

The second stanza of the 'Authors request' should also be noted on account of the suggestion which it carries that the poet and the Phoenix were separated by a wide gulf in social rank:

> Some deepe-read scholler fam'd for Poetrie,
> Whose wit-enchanting verse deserueth fame,
> Should sing of thy perfections passing beautie,
> And eleuate thy famous worthy name:
>   Yet I the least, and meanest in degree,
>   Endeuoured haue to please in praising thee.

[1] Dr. Grosart (p. xxii) is certainly right in taking these lines to mean that Chester 'was not pleading for himself but [for] another'. On the other hand, the poet does not plead with the Phoenix to accept the Turtle-dove, but expresses satisfaction over what is already an accomplished fact.

The language and the tone of Chester's 'Request', then, make it almost certain that he was addressing the Phoenix as his patroness and not as the object of his affections. Accordingly, the employment of the first person in the 'Cantoes'—if, indeed, these were written by Chester—may be regarded as merely a literary device adopted by the poet to enable him to give lyrical expression to his theme.[1]

If, now, we proceed, as I think we may, on the assumption that in *Loves Martyr* the Turtle and Phoenix stand for a real man and woman, it becomes our problem to determine if possible the persons whom Chester had in mind. This is necessarily a more difficult problem, and perhaps one which it may be impossible to solve with perfect certainty. For Chester has woven into the poem many obscure allusions, the key to which is to be gained only through intimate acquaintance with the biographies of the persons concerned. The explanation of the allegory which is proposed in the following paragraphs must therefore be considered in many points as conjecture rather than established fact. All that can be claimed is that it fits the facts so far as we know them. But with the present state of our knowledge many allusions in the poem are still unexplained.

In the preceding section it has been shown that Robert Chester the poet was a dependant of Sir John Salusbury, and that he had a close acquaintance with affairs in the household at Lleweni. It will be remembered, also, that the very poem which we are at present considering was dedicated to Sir John, who was, so far as we know, the poet's only

---

[1] It is to be noted that the 'Cantoes Alphabet-wise' are declared to be 'made by the Paphian Doue'. This may mean that Chester essayed to write in the person of the Paphian Dove, or it may be that these Cantos were really composed by the 'Turtle-dove' (i. e. according to the theory which will be advanced later, by Sir John Salusbury). One recalls in this connexion the pieces appended by Salusbury in the Parry volume, which like *Loves Martyr* was dedicated to him as patron. On the other hand, at the end of the 'Cantoes verbally written', which follow those 'made by the Paphian Doue', we find Chester's name subscribed (*Loves Martyr*, p. 167); and in these as in the others the *Turtle-dove* speaks in his own person.

Introduction

patron. Accordingly, if Chester intended his allegory to celebrate the love and marriage of two real persons, it appears most likely that those persons were Sir John Salusbury and his wife.

The marriage of Salusbury and Ursula Stanley occurred in December, 1586, only three months after the execution of Thomas Salusbury. According to all accounts, John Salusbury was deeply affected by his brother's tragic death. Indeed, in a 'poysie' composed for the wedding festivities the hope is expressed that his marriage might serve 'to delighte hys doulfull mynde'.[1] This fits well, it will be observed, with the dejection in which the Phoenix finds the Turtle-dove at her first meeting with him.[2] This dejection, upon which Chester lays much stress, is the result, as we are expressly told, of a bereavement. Unfortunately, in the stanza in which the Turtle-dove gives the reason for his melancholy there is some confusion in the text which plainly requires emendation. If we emend the second line as has been suggested[3] the text becomes consistent and the stanza is rendered perfectly intelligible:

> My teares are for my *Turtle* that is dead,
> My sorrow springs from his want that is gone,
> My heauy note sounds for the soule that's fled,
> And I will dye for him left all alone:
>   I am not liuing, though I seeme to go,
>   Already buried in the graue of wo.

It may be remarked, further, that when the cause of the Turtle-dove's sorrow is thus understood the sympathetic offers of the Phoenix:

> Mine eyes shall answer teare for teare of thine:
> Sigh thou, Ile sigh, &c.,

and,

>   I will beare
> Halfe of the burdenous yoke thou dost sustaine,

---

[1] See below, p. 36.   [2] *Loves Martyr*, pp. 123-6.
[3] See above, p. lviii, note.

are more appropriate than if the mourning were made for the loss of a previous mate.[1]

Ursula Stanley, though born of an illegitimate connexion, was the daughter of an illustrious nobleman who boasted the double title, Earl of Derby and King of Man. In Danielle's verses her lineage is mentioned with evident pride:

> ffrom princely blood & Ryale stocke she came
> of egles brood hatcht in a loftie nest.[2]

And similarly in the 'poysie' presented on the occasion of her marriage to Salusbury she is referred to as 'A princlye byrde'.[3] In this connexion it is to be observed that *Loves Martyr* contains more than one intimation that the Phoenix was born of noble family. In his 'request to the Phœnix' Chester refers to her 'famous worthy name'; and in the 'Conclusion' he announces the birth of the Phoenix's heir in these words:

> *Another* princely Phœnix vpright stood.

Again in the *Loves Martyr* this princely Phoenix, born of the union of the Turtle and Phoenix, is explicitly referred to as a female. This agrees with the record of births in the Salusbury family. The eldest child was Jane, who was born October, 1587.

So far as the Phoenix is concerned, then, the interpretation of the allegory which is here proposed appears to offer no difficulties. It remains to inquire whether the description of the Turtle-dove can be applied to Sir John Salusbury.

Before taking up the question directly it should be noted that an undoubted allusion to Salusbury is introduced in the

---

[1] Stanza 19 of the 'Cantoes Alphabet-wise', which begins:
> Thou art a *Turtle* wanting of thy mate,

cannot be cited as evidence on the question under discussion, for the reason that this stanza, as the context shows, is addressed to the Phoenix and not to the Turtle-dove.

[2] See below, p. 31.

[3] See below, p. 37.

stanzas on the lion.¹ These stanzas are strikingly similar in tone to the 'Poore sheapheards Profecye', one of the pieces in the Christ Church MS.,² in which Chester sings Salusbury's praise under the figure of a white lion—the arms of the Salusbury family. In both the lion is represented as worried by beasts of baser kind, and in both his eventual vengeance upon his enemies is confidently predicted. The general resemblance between the 'Profecye' and the description of the lion in *Loves Martyr* is in itself sufficient to lead one to suspect that they relate to the same person. But in addition to this the stanzas in *Loves Martyr* contain a direct reference to Salusbury in the words:

> He neuer wrongs a man nor hunts his pray,
> If they will yeeld submissiue at his feete.

The personal allusion in these lines is at once perceived when one notes Mrs. Thrale's statement that for generations the motto of the Salusburys was, *Satis est prostrasse leoni*. A similar allusion, it is to be observed, occurs in the concluding lines of Griffith's verses on the Salusbury motto:

> But such as comes from Noble Lyons race,
> (like this braue Squire) who yeeldes, recyues to grace.³

The discovery of this allusion to Salusbury in these stanzas on the lion does not, of course, determine the interpretation of the allegory of the Turtle-dove. Nevertheless, it supplies an additional bit of evidence of the close relation in which the poet stood to his patron. The very mention of the lion in his catalogue of beasts was sufficient, it would appear, to turn Chester's thoughts to the white lion of Lleweni, and accordingly he digresses to introduce stanzas in honour of his patron.

In one remarkable passage in *Loves Martyr* Chester drops his figure for the moment and gives us a description of the

---

¹ *Loves Martyr*, p. 112.   ² See below, pp. 20–21.
³ See below, p. 33.

Turtle-dove not as a bird but as a man. Since it is in this human portrait that we may most reasonably expect to find the clue to the identity of the Turtle-dove, I quote the passage in question, asking the reader to note that the last stanza expressly identifies the person here described with the Turtle-dove:

> Hard by a running streame or crystall fountaine,
> Wherein rich *Orient* pearle is often found,
> Enuiron'd with a high and steepie mountaine,
> A fertill soile and fruitful plot of ground,
> There shalt thou find true *Honors* louely *Squire*,
> That for this *Phœnix* keepes *Prometheus* fire.
>
> His bower wherein he lodgeth all the night,
> Is fram'd of Cædars and high loftie Pine,
> I made his house to chastice thence despight,
> And fram'd it like this heauenly roofe of mine:
> His name is *Liberall honor*, and his hart,
> Aymes at true faithfull seruice and desart.
>
> Looke on his face, and in his browes doth sit,
> Bloud and sweete *Mercie* hand in hand vnited,
> Bloud to his foes, a president most fit
> For such as haue his gentle humour spited:
> His Haire is curl'd by nature mild and meeke,
> Hangs carelesse downe to shrowd a blushing cheeke.
>
> Giue him this Ointment to annoint his Head,
> This precious Balme to lay vnto his feet,
> These shall direct him to this *Phœnix* bed,
> Where on a high hill he this Bird shall meet:
> And of their Ashes by my doome shal rise,
> Another *Phœnix* her to equalize.[1]

Several points in these lines suggest that the subject of this description is Sir John Salusbury. In the first place the landscape agrees with that of Lleweni, which was situated in the fertile meadows bordering the river Clwyd, and environed by hills and mountains. Again in the phrase 'louely Squire' Chester uses a term which was definitely descriptive

---

[1] *Loves Martyr*, pp. 11–12.

Introduction

of Salusbury's rank until he was knighted in June, 1601—and there can be no doubt that *Loves Martyr* was composed before this date. Compare in this connexion Griffith's reference to Salusbury as 'this braue Squire'.[1] Significant also in the description is the reference to 'Bloud and sweete *Mercie* hand in hand vnited', which finds a parallel in Griffith's characterization of Salusbury:

> Of Might to spoyle, but yett of Mercie spare.
> A Symbole sure to Salsberie due by right:
> who [2] still doth ioyne, his Mercie with his Might.

Moreover, Chester himself in his ' Poore sheapheards Profecye ' stresses this same combination of gentleness and fierceness in Salusbury:

> A milke whight Lion that betokned mercye,

is the opening line, but a little later Chester declares:

> A time shall come when as this Lion rores
> The poore lame foxe will hide him in a hole
> And all his petie ffreinds wil be Amazd
> And dare not peepe for feare.[3]

Finally, it is to be noted that these stanzas in *Loves Martyr* not only give a picture of the Turtle-dove but also give him a name:

> His name is *Liberall honor*.

Here if anywhere, one feels, a definite clue to his identity must be intended. In his poems in the Christ Church MS. Chester has shown a fondness for acrostics; may it not be that here he resorted to an anagram? Out of ' Liberall honor' I can make nothing, but if one take instead the Latin equivalent, *Honos liberalis*, the letters will be found to spell IOHON SALLSBERI. If this be accidental it is at least a curious coincidence. The spelling ' Sallsberi ', it may be granted, does not occur elsewhere, though in Griffith's line on the

---

[1] See below, p. 32. [2] MS. whose. [3] See below, p. 21.

motto, *Posse et Nolle Nobile*, one finds 'Salsberie'; and when the laxity of Elizabethan spelling is considered, exactness cannot be insisted upon. Moreover, one can easily understand that the necessity of arranging the letters of Salusbury's name to form words yielding some fitting sense may have compelled some latitude in the orthography. 'Honos liberalis' is perhaps a pedantic and strained anagram, but it must be remembered that we are dealing with a poet who was capable of even more desperate expedients. When Chester found himself troubled to fit 'Great Britain' into the rhyme-scheme of his stanza, he evaded the difficulty by writing instead 'large *Britanicus*', and placing in the margin an apologetic 'Rithmi gratia'.[1] With such a glaring instance of unpoetic licence before us, we are hardly justified in rejecting the possibility of the Salusbury anagram in 'Liberall honor' merely because the device impresses us as somewhat far-fetched.

It is barely possible also that personal names may be concealed in the catalogues of plants, fishes, precious stones, &c., which make up a large part of Dame Nature's instruction of the Phoenix. One recalls the employment of flower-names to form acrostics in Chester's 'Wynter Garland',[2] as well as the similar use of precious stones in the Parry volume.[3] Either these catalogues must be regarded as extreme examples of pedantic irrelevance or they mean more than meets the eye, though any esoteric meaning which they may contain has been effectually concealed, at least from *my* 'dull Imagination'.[4]

In representing the Turtle-dove as having his home in 'Paphos Ile',[5] Chester seems to have in mind no definite

[1] *Loves Martyr*, p. 28.

[2] See below, Christ Church Poems, No. X.

[3] *Posie* 6.

[4] See Chester's preliminary admonition, 'To those of light beleefe,' *Loves Martyr*, p. 15.

[5] Thus, see p. 9, stanza 4; p. 24, stanzas 1 and 4; p. 81, stanza 1; p. 101, stanza 4; p. 113, stanza 2.

topographical allusion. Paphos cannot be identified with Great Britain, for the reason that Nature describes the cities of England long before she arrives with her charge at the Isle which is their destination. So far as I can see, Paphos was chosen by the poet solely on account of its mythological association with Venus. The case is different with the 'high hill' on which the Phoenix is represented as first meeting the Turtle-dove. Here, it would seem, the poet must have in mind a definite place, presumably the place at which Salusbury and Ursula Stanley were married. But I do not know where this marriage took place, and consequently am unable to offer any suggestion as to the high hill.

If the interpretation of Chester's allegory proposed in the preceding paragraphs be accepted, it follows that *Loves Martyr*—or at least that portion of it which is concerned with the story of the Turtle and Phoenix—must have been written more than a decade before its publication in 1601. Salusbury was married in December, 1586, and his eldest child, Jane, was born in October, 1587. Harry, the next child, was born in September, 1589, but the poem makes no reference to any male issue of the Turtle and Phoenix as might perhaps be expected if it had been composed after this date—although one readily sees that the birth of a second child would have been difficult to reconcile with the allegory of the Phoenix.

There appears to be nothing improbable, however, in supposing a considerable interval between the composition of *Loves Martyr* and its publication. Attention has already been called to the fact that the 'Life of King Arthur' was probably inserted into the poem by Chester as an afterthought. The 'honourable-minded Friends' who 'intreated' him to add the Life of Arthur[1] are apparently the same persons to whom he refers in the opening sentence of his Epistle Dedicatorie: 'Honorable Sir, hauing according to the directions of some of my best-minded friends, finished my

[1] See *Loves Martyr*, p. 34.

lxx   *Poems by Sir John Salusbury and Robert Chester*

long expected labour,' &c. From this one may surmise that the King Arthur section was added not long before the volume's publication. However this may be, we have Chester's word for it that *Loves Martyr* was his 'long expected labour', and this accords well with the supposition that the poem was composed a number of years before its appearance in print in 1601.

In concluding this discussion of the allegory in *Loves Martyr*, a word ought to be said in regard to the Turtle and Phoenix as they appear in the 'Poeticall Essaies' appended to the volume by the greater Elizabethans. This is a matter which thus far has been rigorously excluded from our discussion for the reason that these supplementary pieces manifestly could in no way have influenced the treatment of the allegory by Chester. On the other hand, Chester's poem certainly furnished the suggestion, and to some extent served as the basis, for the allegory in the 'Poeticall Essaies'. To consider in detail the pieces contributed by these five poets particularly the one by Shakspere—would lead us too far afield. Accordingly, I confine myself to noting a few points in which these later poems appear to show a direct connexion with the allegory in *Loves Martyr*.

In the first place one should note carefully the preliminary 'Invocatio' and the stanzas addressed 'To the worthily honor'd Knight Sir Iohn Salisburie' by the 'Vatum Chorus'. In the Invocation the poets 'sustend' their 'mutuall palmes, prepar'd to gratulate / An *honorable friend*'; and in their address to Salusbury they declare that they have been moved to write by 'a true Zeale, borne in our spirites / Responsible to your high Merites'.

> *These were the Parents to our seuerall Rimes,*
> *Wherein* Kind, Learned, Enuious, *al may view,*
> *That we haue writ worthy our selues and you.*

These lines—especially the last—suggest that Sir John Salusbury was not only the person to whom the 'Essaies' were dedicated, like the contributions in a modern *Festschrift*, but that he was also the subject of them.

When we turn to the 'Essaies' themselves we note the tone of friendly regard in which several of the poets refer to the Turtle-dove, as to a familiar acquaintance. Particularly is this the case with Ben Jonson. 'We propose', he writes, ' a person like our *Doue* / Grac'd with a *Phœnix* loue'; and he launches forthwith into a panegyric upon the beauty of this lady. From this theme he returns to pay a tribute to the moral character of the Turtle in these words :

> What sauage, brute Affection,
> Would not be fearefull to offend a *Dame*
>   Of this excelling frame ?
> Much more a noble and right generous *Mind*,
>   (To vertuous moodes enclin'd)
> That knowes the weight of *Guilt* : He will refraine
>   From thoughts of such a straine :
> And to his *Sence* obiect this Sentence euer,
> ' *Man may securely sinne, but safely neuer.*'

Without multiplying quotations, it is clear that to Jonson both Turtle and Phœnix were living persons—man and wife—with whom he stood on terms of acquaintance, perhaps even friendship. It will be remembered in this connexion that in the Salusbury MS. at Christ Church is bound a sheet containing verses written and signed by Jonson's own hand. The presence of this sheet among the papers of the Salusbury family carries an interesting suggestion of a friendship existing between Sir John Salusbury and Jonson.

Marston's contribution differs from all the others in singing the praises ' of a most exact wondrous creature, arising out of the Phœnix and Turtle Doues ashes'. This creature was, of course, the 'princely Phœnix' whose birth Chester announced in his ' Conclusion '. But Marston's lines supply a valuable bit of chronological evidence. This creature, he informs us, ' now is growne vnto maturitie.' In this statement we find positive confirmation of the opinion expressed above, that a number of years intervened between the composition of Chester's poem and its publication. Moreover, Marston's reference to the daughter of the Phoenix and Turtle as grown to maturity fits perfectly with the Salusbury family history, for in 1601 Jane, the eldest child of Sir John, had arrived at the age of fourteen. Marston and Salusbury, it may be added, were both Middle Templers, and it is possible that their acquaintance had its origin in this common connexion.

Shakspere differs essentially in his treatment of the allegory from the other members of the 'Chorus Vatum' and also from Robert Chester. Some of Shakspere's lines, it is true, as Dr. A. H. R. Fairchild has noted,[1] betray the direct influence of passages in *Loves Martyr*, particularly the speech of the Pellican. But starting with these definite suggestions, Shakspere chose to develop his theme along a widely diverging line. In his poem the note from first to last is funereal. A Requiem is sung for the Phoenix and Turtle; and over the urn which encloses their ashes is pronounced a Threnos, concluding:

> To this vrne let those repaire,
> That are either true or faire,
> For these dead Birds sigh a prayer.

Again, though the central point in the myth of the Phoenix is the resurrection from the ashes, Shakspere holds out no such hope for either Phoenix or Turtle:

> Death is now the *Phœnix* nest,
> And the *Turtles* loyall brest,
> To eternitie doth rest.
>
> Leauing no posteritie,
> Twas not their infirmitie
> It was married Chastitie.

---

[1] 'The Phœnix and Turtle. A Crit. and Hist. Interpretation,' *Engl. Stud.*, xxxiii. 377.

Introduction lxxiii

This last stanza is especially remarkable, for it flatly contradicts Marston and Chester, both of whom, as we have seen, give account of a fair creature which issued from the ashes of the Phoenix.

To reconcile Shakspere's allegory either with *Loves Martyr* or with the other 'Poetical Essaies' is thus manifestly impossible. Also, besides these contradictions in matters of fact, his lines contrast sharply with the other poems in their detached and impersonal tone. One searches in vain for any such familiarity as is displayed in Ben Jonson's reference to 'our Doue'. The Turtle and Phoenix are declared 'Co-supremes and starres of Loue', but their love is set forth in abstract and philosophical terms. Indeed, in spite of its ingenuity and its epigrammatic brilliance, the poem as a whole impresses one as frigid and perfunctory.

This may be accounted for, in part, by the conventionality of the figures which Shakspere employs, most of which were borrowed, as Dr. Fairchild shows, from the Court of Love poems. But this, one feels, is only a partial explanation. Shakspere was quite capable of infusing life and warmth into conventional forms. Moreover, the question remains: Why did he choose such a conventional form in a poem written 'to gratulate an honorable friend'? The answer which readily suggests itself is, that Shakspere's relations with Sir John Salusbury were less close than those of Jonson, Marston, and Chapman, so that his lines on the Phoenix and Turtle were a matter of courteous compliance rather than a tribute to a personal friend. The complete absence of personal allusion which one notes with surprise in Shakspere's contribution is satisfactorily explained only on this hypothesis. In any case it is clear, I believe, that in seeking to interpret the allegory which forms the subject of *Loves Martyr* and its appended pieces the inquiry does not begin, but rather ends, with Shakspere's poem. It was Robert Chester, the friend and dependant of Sir John Salusbury, who related in detail the story of the Phoenix and Turtle's love, to which the pieces by Shakspere and his fellows form merely a brief appendix; and it is in Chester's poem that personal allusions appear most distinctly. To judge Chester's allegory on the basis of Shakspere's lines is therefore a reversal of orderly method, which requires that the 'Poeticall Essaies' shall be interpreted in the light of *Loves Martyr*.

Poems

by

Sir John Salusbury, Robert Chester,

and others,

CONTAINED IN MS. 184, IN THE LIBRARY OF

CHRIST CHURCH, OXFORD

I.

Not to extoll your beautie, or sett forth [fol. 34]
your plenteous graces, and your vertues woorth
my yonge Muse dares attempt: such higher skill
belonges vnto a farr more learned qwill:
I only in humble layes endevor here 5
to tell the loue I beare to you (my deare)
and to perswade therin your sweet consent;
" so farr affection makes me eloquent;
you knowe your owne desert; I need not tell it:
you knowe my loue; I cannot then conceale it. 10
When first vnto your all-comandinge eyes
I offred vp my self a sacrifice,
and in the inchantment of your sugred smyle
did myne owne sowle of liberty begwyle:
I found my self to barren of desert, 15
which to supply, I vow'd a constant heart
shold ever honor you with all respects;
" perfect goodwill makes perfect all defects:
this totall summe I tendred then to you,
and still you haue it; (for it is your due) 20
and still shall haue it whiles I liue; vnles
smooth-slydinge Thamisis haue back regresse,
from louely London, to the learned Towne:
or that the loftiest English mountayns crowne
be lowe avayled to a vally deepe. 25
But what avayles me that my vowes I keepe?
yf (as of late) you study to neglect,
and doe despise my dutyfull respect.
I must confesse your liberall grace to me,
outstript my merit; and did make me see 30
my self a debtor in my best habilitie.
But wherof shold arise your mutabilitie?
yf of my self; ô lett me see wherin,

that I may dy for pennance of that sinne;
But yf of you; I thinke it wondrous strange,   35
so choyce a beauty shold delight in change:
the purest colour is a perfect one;
if it be mixt the beauty then is gone:
the lightest, bryghtest, tincture (well you wott)
paynted on whyte, appeares but as a spott.   40
But not of me, nor of your self (I knowe)
this sad dislike of late beginnes to growe,
But of an envie that from my good speed,   [fol. 34ᵇ]
into an others base sowle doth proceede:
your mayde I meane; she (haply) doth invade you,   45
and with her sluttish reasons wold perswade you,
to change your mynd; yet you I knowe are wise,
to sift such malice out of false disguyse:
and neede not feare so vile a thinge as she
a blemish in your high repute can bee;   50
for yf you did you might prevent the ill;
"the absent eare will cause the tongue be still;
"the absent eye keepes knowledge from the mynd;
"she'es chast, that's chary; all the world is blynde
"in sable shadow of the silent night;   55
"all things discerned in the blabbinge light.
Is not your mayd (I pray) at your dispose?
you neede not doubt: for hence the comfort growes,
that when you please she must haue winges to fly;
"the cause remou'd th'effect of force must dye.   60
my Deare, your wisdome must your self direct,
to stopp fames mouth, and blynd the worlds suspect.
which in my Iudgement you can never doe,
as longe as such vile drosse shall censure you;
But vnto you I wholy do remitte   65
the sight herof, and what herin is fitt.

              Your once, instantly, ever,

                    J. S.

II.

[fol. 35]

A dietary for those who have weak backs, in 4-line stanzas (*abcb*), beginning :—

Good sir yf you lack the strengthe in your back.

III.

[fol. 40ᵃ]

GENIUS, where art thou ? I should vse
   thy present ayde; Spirit, Invention,
Wake; and put on the wings of Pindars Muse
      to toure with my Intention
  high as his mind, that doth aduance   5
her vpright head aboue the reach of Chance
      or the times Envy:
     Pythius; I apply
my flowing numbers to thy golden Lyre;
      O, then Inspire   10
thy Preist in this strange rapture; heat my Brayne
      with Delphique fier
that I may sing my thoughts in some vnvulga*re* strayne.

Rich Beame of honor, shed yo*ur* Light
On these darke Rimes; that o*ur* Affection   15
may shine through euery Chinke, to euery sight
      graced by yo*ur* Reflection.
Then shall o*ur* verses (like strong Charmes)
Breake the knit Circle of her stony Armes
      that curbes yo*ur* spirit,   20
     and keepes yo*ur* merit
lockt in her cold Embraces, from the view
      of Eyes more trew,
who would with Iudgment search, searching, conclude
      (as proou'd in you)   25
Trew Noblesse Palme growes strayght, though handled
      ne're so Rude.

Nor thinke your selfe vnfortunate
If subiect to the Iealous Errors
Of Politique pretext that swayes a state ;
    Sinke not beneath these terrors :   30
But whisper, O glad Innocence
When only a mans birth is his offence,
    or the disfauor
    of such, as sauor
nothing but practise vpon Honors thrall ;   35
    O Vertues fall,
when thy white Essence (like the Anatomy
    in Surgeans hall)
Is but a Statists theame, to read Phlebotomy.
                    [fol. 40ᵇ]

Let Brontes, and Blacke Steropes   40
    sweat at the forge, theyre hammers beating ;
An hower will come they must affect theyre Ease
    though but while mettall's heating :
And (after all theyre Ætnæan Ire)
Gold that is perfect will out liue the fire.   45
    for fury wasteth
    as Patience lasteth ;
No Armor to the mind ; he is shott-free
    from Iniury,
that is not hurt ; not he that is not hit   50
    So fooles we see
oft scape theyre Imputation more through lucke then
                        Wit.

But to your selfe most Loyall Lord
    whose heart in that bright Sphere flames clearest,
(though many Gems be in your bosome stor'd   55
    vnknowne which is the dearest)
If I auspiciously diuine
(as my hope tells) that our drad Cynthia's shine
    shall light those places
    with lustrous graces,   60

where Darknesse with her gloomy-sceptred hand
　　　　　doth now command;
Ô then (our best-best-lou'd) let me Importune
　　　　　that you will stand
As far from all Reuolt as you are now from fortune.　65

B. Jo.

Nec te quaesiueris extra

I am indebted to Mr. Percy Simpson of Oxford, who is engaged in editing Jonson's Works for the Clarendon Press, for the following note on this poem: 'Printed in the 1640 Folio of Jonson's Works, with the title, "An Ode to Iames Earle of Desmond, writ in Queene Elizabeth's time, since lost, and recovered." This was James Fitzgerald, the "Tower Earl", born 1570 (?), died 1601. His father, the 15th earl, had been declared a traitor and was killed in 1583. In 1586 an Act of Parliament declared the estates forfeited. The son, who had been given up to the English Government, was kept a close prisoner till 1600; he was then sent to Ireland with instructions to bring over the Geraldine faction. He failed, and returned to England. He had merely been used as a pawn by the Government.'

IV.

Of late I went my dearest deare to trie her,　　　　[fol. 41ᵃ]
And found her sleeping, & then began to woe her,
And safelie stouping gentlie laid me by her
And still my mistress slept, but did not sleepe,

And then I tought my wanton eye to gaze　　　5
one head, on face, one feet, on legges on thighe
where sweet delight remaines, I sawe the place
and still my mistress sawe, but wold not see

And then I tought my toung to blaze my paine
and softlie whispering tould her in her eare　　　10
both of my loue and of her proud disdaine
and still my mistress hard but would not heare

Then I tought mine armes her neck to foulde
and of a gentle kisse did her beguile
Soe kist and kist till kissing made me bould   15
and still my m*istres*s smilde but wold not smile [1]

And then I tought my Idle fingers woe
each comelie p*art*e from head vnto the heele
where Cupid holdes his campe I touched toe
and still my m*istres*s felt, but wold not feele   20

And the*n* I tought my man to wantonnise
And in the boate of true delight to Roe
of true delights, not Idle fantasies
And still my m*istres*s did, but wold not doe

> But since she slepte & smilde & felt and did in deed
> I wish I might be oftner soe beguild   26
> Thoughe not in shoue
> The substaunce I effect let shadowes goe.

Finis.

[Two initials, possibly ' J. S.', much flourished over.]

V.

Bewties delite geve place to this fayer starr   [fol. 43]
loocke still one her, hur eyes will geve yow light
A m*m*iabel she is hur lovely fame goes farre
n umber her vertues and behould her sight
C ompare her then to any that is livinge   5
h ur bewety w*i*th ther bewty wilbe strivinge
w ine colored cheke tournd to a cherye red

---

[1] MS. smilde.

y eldes comfort to the eye that doth behould her
n atur with hvr sweet bewty now is fedd
n ote but hur lyvely partes when you vnfould hur   10
    And yow will saye that Venus shoud her coninge
    And in hur face trve bewty sate a-soninge

        Finis. J. Salusburye
              made in marche 1598.

At the top of fol. 43ᵃ, and likewise at the top of fol. 87ᵇ, is written the word 'Emanuell'. Cf. also 'Iessv' which stands in Christ Church MS. 183, at the top of fol. 41ᵃ. The practice of heading a page with some form of the sacred name appears to have been frequent; see *Hist. MSS. Commission, Report on MSS. of Lord Middleton* (1911), p. 592.

VI.

B ewty a bane yet blessing vnto many
l ovelie desire being plased in their thought
a nd the true forme of love being ment of any
n oe way to pretious or to deare is bought
    C onstant in word in thought in hart in dead   5
    h eapes twenty thousand blessings in loves steede
w ater your harts with true religious love
y ow that intend loves love to be estemed
n othinge so sower as vnkynd to proue
n or nothing sweeter faithfull to be deemed   10
    o beare in mind love is a holy thing
    not to be hated by a mighty king.

        Finis Robert chester
             made in march 1598.

The person named in the acrostics seems to be Blanche, daughter of John Vaughn of Blaen-y-Cwm, who married Edward Wynn of Ystrad, son of Morys Wynn of Gwydir and his wife Catherine of Berain. See Sir John Wynne, *History of the Gwydir Family*, Oswestry, 1878, Table III (facing p. 49). Note also the occurrence in Christ Church MS. 183 (fol. 33ᵃ) of verses by Edward Wynn.

VII.

Yt was the time when silly Bees colde speake [fol. 43ᵇ]
And in that time I was a sillye Bee
Who suckt on time vntill my hart did breake
Yet neuer founde the time wold fauour me
  of all the swarme I only colde not thriue,   5
   Yet brought I waxe and hony to the hiue

Then this I buzde when time noe sappe wolde giue
Why ys this blessed time to me soe drye
Syth in this time the lasye drone doth liue
The waspe, the worme, the gnatt, the butterflye   10
  Mated with greefe I kneeled on my knees
   And thus complained to the king of Bees.

God graunt my liege thy time may neuer end
and yet vouchssaffe to heare my plaint of time
which every fruitles flye hath found a freind   15
and I cast downe when Atomies doe clime
  The king replide but this, peace peeuish Bee
   Th'art borne to searue the time, the time not thee

The time not thee, this word clipt short my wings
and made me wormelike stoope that once did flye   20
A foule Regard disputeth not with kings
Receaueth a Repulse and asks not why
  Then from the time a time I me withdrewe
   to feed on Henbaine, hemlocks, nettle, Rue.

[1] But from these leaues noe dramme of sweet I draine   25
my headstrong fortunes did my witts bewitch

---

[1] This stanza is written on the margin and marked for insertion at this point.

the ioyce dispearst black blood in euery vaine
for hony galle for waxe I gathered pitch
    my combe a rifte, my hiue a leafe must be   29
    soe chaingde that Bees scarce take me for a Bee.

I worke on weedes when Moone is in the wane
whilst all the swarme in sonneshine tast the Rose
on blackroote fearne I feed and suck my bane
Whilst on the Eglantine the rest repose
    Having too much they still repine for more   35
    and cloyde with sweetnes surfeit in their store.

Swolne fatt with feasts full merely they passe
In sweetned clusters falling on a tree
Wheare finding me to nible on the grasse
some scorne, some muse, and some doe pitty me   40
    And some in Enuy whisper to the king
    Some must be still, and some must haue no stinge.

Are bees waxt waspes, and spiders to afflict
Do honie bowels make the spiritts gall
Is this the Ioyce of flowers to stirre suspect   45
Ist not Inough to tread on them that fall
    What sting hath patience but a sighing greefe
    That stings nought but yt selfe without reliefe

True patience the provender for fooles,   [fol. 44]
Sadd patience that wayteth at the dore,   50
Patience that learnes thus to conclude in scooles,
Patient am I, therefore I must be poore
    Great king of Bees that righteth every wrong,
    Lysten to patience in her dying song.

I cannot feed on fennell like some flyes,   55
Nor flye to every flower to gather gaine,

My appetyte waites on my princes eyes,
Contented with contempt, and pleasde with paine,
    And yet expecting of An happy hower,
    when he may say this Bee shall sucke A flower   60

Of all the greefes that most my patience grate,
thers one that fretteth in the highest degree,
To se some Caterpilleres breed of late,
Cropping the fflowers that shold sustaine the Bee,
    Yet smiled I, for that the wysest knowes   65
    That moathes will eate the cloth, cankar the Rose.

Once did I soe by fflying in the ffield,
ffowle beastes to browze vppon the lyllye ffaire,
vertue nor bewtie cold no succour yeld,
Alls provender for Asses but the ayre,   70
    The parciall world of this takes lyttle heed,
    To give them flowers that shold one thilstles feed.

Tis only I must draine Egiptian flowers,
having no savour, bytter sappe they haue,
and seeke out rotten tombes and dead mens bowers,   75
to bight on petoes growing on the graue,
    Yf this I cannot haue, yett haples Bee,
    Wishing Tobacco I will fly to thee.

What thoughe yt dye my longes in deepest black,
A mourning habitt suites A sable hart,   80
what thoughe the fume sound memory doe crack,
forgettfulnes is fittest for my smart,
    A verteous fume[1] lett it be carude in oke,
    That words, hopes, wittes and all the world is smoke.

ffive yeares twice tould with promises perfumd,   85
my hope-stufte head was cast into A slumber,

---

[1] MS. *has been corrected from* sinne; *the reading is not certain.*

Sweet dreames on gold, on dreames I then presumde,
And mongst the Bees thought I was in the number :
  Waking I ffound hive-hopes had made me vaine
  Twas not Tobacco stupefied the braine.   90

Ingenium, nummos, studium, spem, tempus, Amicos cum male perdiderem [sic] *perdere verba leue.*[1]

  This Apologue of the Bee expresses in bitter terms the discontent of the Earl of Essex after he fell out of favour with Queen Elizabeth. It was composed either by Essex himself (as is stated in some MSS.) or by his secretary, Henry Cuff. Copies of the poem occur also in the following MSS. : Brit. Mus. Addit. 5495, fol. 28ᵇ-29ᵃ; 5956, fol. 23ᵇ ; Egerton MS. 923, fol. 5ᵇ; Harley MSS. 2127, fol. 58 ; 6910, fol. 167 ; 6947, fol. 230 ; Caius Coll. Cambridge MS. 73, fol. 157 ; Tanner MS. 76, fol. 93-94 ; Ashmole MSS. 781, fol. 132-4, and 767, fol. 1-3 (fourteen stanzas only). The first three stanzas of the piece were printed by John Dowland in his *Third Book of Songs or Airs* (1603), from which they have been reprinted by E. Arber, *English Garner*, iv (1882), 620-1, and by A. H. Bullen, *Shorter Elizabethan Poems*, pp. 128-9. This poem has been printed in *Pieces of Ancient Poetry*, Bristol, 1814, p. 25, in J. Park's edition of Walpole's *Royal and Noble Authors*, ii. 109-12, and by Grosart, *Miscell. of the Fuller Worthies Library*, iv, No. 3, pp. 85-9.

VIII.

D ay glorefying Phœbe doth arise   [fol. 44ᵇ]
O pening her christall colowred gates of bewty
R ose Coloured cheeks starre bewtefying eyes
O mnipotent deuinenes owes thee dutye.
T he graces at thy rare Natiuety   5
H overd about thy head with siluer wings
Y elding a flowry chaplet fit for kings

[1] The Latin elegiacs are written on the margin of the page in the hand of fol. 43ᵇ.

H ate at thy birthday was a banisht slaue
A nd bewty like a prisner was thy thrall
L oue like a captiue crept from forth his graue   10
S wearing to be a seruaunt at thy call.
A nd Cupid on his knees to thee did fall:
L etting the world to know: that on his knee
L owe bending honor stooped vnto thee.

IX.

D iana in thy bosome plast her bower
O ffring vp incens to soe fair a Sainct
R itch Nature on thy browe hath built her tower
O utbrauing Venus with a looke soe quaint
T hy feature great Apelles colde not paint   5
H is cunning workemanship was to to base
I n painting of thy rare accomplisht face
E ternall honor wolde his art disgrase.

H ow blessed is the partner of thy bedd
A ttayning such a wonder in his armes   10
L oue-greetings with thy musky breath is fedd
S weet sugred sleepe thy slumbring eyelidds charmes
A donis sings like to a Nightingall
L oue ditties in thy praise maiesticall

              finis   Robt Chester.

X.

A wynter garland of Sommer [fol. 45ᵃ]
fflowers made in manner of A
Neweyeares gyfte to the Right
Worshipfull John Salusbury
Esqʳ of the body to the
Queenes most exelent
Maiestye
1598.

Cold frosty wynter hauing nipte my penne
and Boreas Isycles nue hanging downe
enforseth wytt and wysedome now and then
to stand in dainger, and to feare the frowne
    of ripe depe knowledge and experience,   5
    that is my refuge and my sure defence,

I charme the coldnesse to forsake my hand,
I coniure vp my spiryttes at this time.
Goodmeaning tells me he my freind will stand,
To vnderprop my tottering rotten ryme   10
    And I being armde with A presumpteous loue,
    from my goodwill disdanefulnes will shoue :

Therefore to thee sole patron of my good,
I proffer vp the proffer of my hart,
my vndeserved favoures vnderstood,   15
to thee and none but thee I will impart :
    O grace them with thy gratious gracing looke
    that in pure kindnes¹ much haue vndertooke

---

¹ MS. this *crossed out.*

                O flattery great bandogge to the poore
                Ile tye thee in an Iron fetterd chaine   20
                Necessety shall goe from dore to dore
                Wheare skueking [1] mysers and fatt churles remaine
                    and feed thee with their crummes, there thow shalt perish
                    thee in my hart fowle monster ile not chearysh

Jelliflower.   A Jelliflowre whose sweet carnatian smell   25
                the hony gathering Bee doth alwaies loue
Daphadill.   seekes to incompasse the sweet Daphadill
                and all her flowring vertues to approue
                    they ioy to growe in gardens both togeather
                    not fearing Boreas wrathfull stormy weather 30

Organy.   Neare vnto theyse doth growe the Organye
Orice.   and Orice that we name the Flowerdeluce
                delighting in each others company
                and in domme sylence doe their loues infuce
                    they water one and other with that dewe   35
                    that in the morning from their leaues doth flowe

Honysuckle.   The Honysuckle honyes only last
Rose.   fills vp the Arboure wheare the Rose doth growe
                and with her spreading braunches hath incompast
                the sharpe growne prickles that this plant doth show
                    they doe embrace and in embracing [2] vowe   41
                    Nature with nature will her force allowe.

Ladies **N**auel. The Ladies Nauell Nauell of delyghte   [fol. 45ᵇ]
                A pleasaunt and delityous lovely plante
Oleander.   And Oleander whose rytch verteous sight   45
                Learned Apothicaries doe often wante
                    bothe theyse do decke my garlands of rytch flowers
                    and bewtefy faire Venus louely bowers.

---

[1] See *Eng. Dial. Dict.* under 'scouk'.   [2] MS. loue *crossed out.*

Christ Church MS.   17

Stickadoue.   The stickadoue that lyes in Ladies brestes
               The gentle pillow to soe faire A plante   50
               scorning to haunt the ravens coleblack nestes
Touchmenot.   And Touchmenot in this kind acte doth pante
                   both freinds, both favoryttes in perfect loue
                   is Touchmenot and kyndly Stickadoue.

               Amidst my lovely arbour there doth growe   55
               the handmaid vnto perfect chastetye
Agnus Castus.   rytch Agnus Castus that the world doth know
               is A great queller of hott luxurye
                   to grace the loving humour of all these
Hartsease.   I found A flower y^t most men call faire Hartsease.

Ladies Seale.   Our Ladies Seale A Seale of perfect bewtie   61
               that adds the waxe vnto the honyed Bee
Yooke Elme.   and Yooke Elme that doth make men owe their dutie
               theise prety plantes in favour doe agree
                   wishing vppon the Elme to set a seale   65
                   that might the moysture of this plant reveale

Venus Look-   Amongst all these is Venus Looking glasse
  ing glasse.   A louely plant to[1] please the gazing eye
Hyacinthus.   and Hyacinthus that doth round incompasse
               this fragraunt flower of maiesty   70
                   the queene of love sole paragon of blysse
                   this faire boy Hyacinthus stole to kysse.

Strawbery.   With these is sett the spreading strawberye
               both redd and whight, not pleasing to the smell
               yet yeldes great comfort to the inward fancy   75
               and for to quench the thirst doth much exell
Angellica.   Angellica the plagues preservatiue
               Lovely and faire mongst these plantes doth thriue.

[1] MS. gaze *crossed out.*

B asill.	And Basill best beloude beloude of many	
	for the rare vertue that yt doth inclose	80
L auander.	and louely Lauander not vnknowne to any	
	smelling in operation like the Rose	
	Basill for Blessednes and blessed ioy	
	and Lauander beloude of Venus boy.	

V irgins bow*er*.	All these do deck A Virgins lovely bower	85
[**S** weet]	and bewtyfie my garland in the spring	
Marierome.	sweet Marierome amongst the*m* beares A power	
	of whom the sheapheards roundelaies doe sing	
	And gathe*r* yt on playing hollydaies	
	that doth reviue ther homely springing ioyes.	90

R osemarye.	Remembring Rosemary that increaseth sence	[fol. 46ᵃ]
	And doth reviue the dulled memory	
[**A** rkeangell].	Arkeangell that doth never make offence	
	but is accounted gentle meeke and lovely	
L adies smock.	O*ur* Ladies smock doth overspread the rest	95
	Vnder the wh*i*ch I sought to builde A nest

	And Last of all to make my garland neate	
Y outhwort.	I placed Youthwort faire Affections lover	
L ady lacies.	And Lady Lacies mongst the*m* tooke A seate	
	And thus I framd faire Venus Lovely bower	100
	Wheare Cupid syttes and still his notes doth shifte	
	Singing thy prayses in A newe Yeares gifte.	

                finis   Rob Chester

XI.

Præcatio

Elizabeth that braunch of perfect blisse
We call our queene for whom we all must pray
raigne golden showers of peace vppon this land
[that she in peace may weare the English crowne][1]
and lett thy Angells lead her vp and downe   5
that she in peace may weare the English crowne
this makes me still to pray vppon my knee
and curst be he that praies not after me
the lord preserve the howse of Salusburye

     Amen Ro Chester

Elizabeth was the name of Sir John Salusbury's sister; see the Introduction, p. xii.

XII.

A poore Sheapheards introduction made in A merrimt of christmas at the house of the Right Worshipfull John Salusbury of Lleweny Esqr Etc.

Sheapheards be sylent and our musick cease
heare duells our frolique freind of Arcady
whose dogges defend our sheep from greedy wolues
whose sheep doth cloth our silly sheapheard swaines
whose oxen tills the grownd that yelds vs corne   5
whose corne doth reliue the fatherles
And fatherles still pray for his relieffe
we of Arcadia sometime frolique swaines
swaines that delight in homely pleasaunt mirth
in due obedience and regard of loue   10
shold heare present as newe yeares homely gifte

[1] MS. *a line drawn through this line.*

peares Apples fildbieres or the hazell nutt
or other fruite that this faire clymatt yelds
but nipping winter and a forward spring
blasted our trees and all our sommer budds 15
whose blossomes shold haue yelded dainty fare
therefore seing all giftes giftes that shold befreind[1] vs
the balesome weather and cold spring denied
In signe of honor and obedience [fol. 46ᵇ]
to the whight Lyon of A r c a d i a 20
that doth defend our liues from ravenous beares
and feeds vs with the pray that he persues
A homely cuntry hornepipe we will daunce
A sheapheards prety Gigg to make him sport
and sing A madringall[2] or roundelay 25
to please our Lordlike sheapheard lord[3] of vs
take hands take hands our hartes lett vs Advaunce
and strive to please his humour with A daunce.

finis Rot Chester

XIII.

A poore sheapheards profecye

A milke whight Lion that betokned mercye
did[4] rainge About A pleasaunt wildernes
where foxes Serpentes and devowring Tygers
The long paude beare and stearne Rinocoros
The fearefull hare and nimble footed Roe 5
The vntamd Oliphant and other beastes
beastes of sterne nature did this Lyon haunt

[1] MS. befreinds.
[2] MS. and *crossed out*.
[3] MS. squier *and then* king *written and crossed out*.
[4] MS. raig *crossed out*.

he often with his kindnes did them nowrish
That Tyger-like his blood did seeke to perish
A limping foxe that still the dogges did haunt 10
barkes[1] at this Lion : and the lordlike beast
Smiles at his follie : O Gentillity
how thow woldst quaile thy folish enemie
A time shall come when as this Lion rores
The poore lame foxe will hide him in a hole 15
And all his petie ffreinds wil be Amazd
And dare not peepe for feare : o misery
When men like beastes[2] are wrought with knavery
As for the rest that are this Lions freinds
hee'le bid them welcome to his Lordlike caue 20
And kill fatt venison to make them merry
Thus ends my Simple Sheapheards profecy
True as my creed though he deferres the time
he'le make the foxe the pillery to clyme
The Lion bids yow welcome once agen 25
And craues his fellow ffreinds to say A m e n.

finis Robt Chetr.

XIV. [fol. 47ᵃ]

A Conceite.

ffowle pried it self breeds envy long
And is A poyson fresh and strong
And by experience it is knowne
To be as marrow in the bone
And those that grow of sundry seeds 5
At last do proue but stinking weeds
And if pure wheat be sowde in tares
The wheat Assuredly it mars.

finis John Salusbury.

---

[1] *Interlined above* braies *crossed out.*
[2] MS. *altered from* beastes like men.

XV.

A Concete to the former.

A base bread haggard that my chaunce doth light
with the Imperious eagle in her flight
and gainst all nature in her nest doth breed
and with the eagles food his yong ons feed:
shall this great grace alter the buzards mind,   5
I it must be for kitt will after kind;
havinge no name but given by the nurse
in basenes[1] borne and now by basenes worse
for having stole A name from gentry,
pried is his coate by lawfull heraldrie   10
base hawtie pried did soe his kindred blott,
that in this fortune he himselfe forgott:
but Joues great bird doth laffe this kight to scorne
to se how priede his basenes had oerborne
and pluck his winges he shall not mount so   15
        highe
but fall into the cave of beggarye.

                finis J. S.

XVI.

Ornatissimo Viro, Summoq⟨ue⟩ Honore   [fol. 47ᵇ]
Dignissimo, Johanni Salusbury Armigero
Carmen gratulatorium.

Vestra meas dignas expectat gratia grates,
At plusquam grat'is gratia digna tua est.
Ergo dabo; sed verba dabo; nam verba supersunt.
At fallunt, dices, qui dare verba solent

---

[1] *Corrected from* baesnes.

Verum est; et quoniam non fallam munera verbis 5
Ipse aliquid plusquam verbula mera dabo;
Carmina nempe dabo: sed sunt haec verba: quid obstat
Verba darem? cum alij vendere verba solent.
    Tuam dignitatem
    Mirifice colens. 10

    Edoauardus d'Otthen.

XVII.

A welcome home   [fol. 48ª]
To the Right Worshipfull John Salusbury
Esqr of the bodie to the Queenes most
Exelent Maiestye

Your eares hauing hard the Nightingall soe long,
I feare will blame my hoarse-throat rauens song:
The swanns that laue their blacke feet in the streames,
Haue in their sweetnes sang you golden theames:
[1] Court-bewtefying Poets in their verse, 5
Homerian like sweete stanzoes did rehearse:
Then blame not my homebred vnpollisht witt,
That in the Nightowles cabinet doe sitt:
Yf that my lines be blunt, or harsh, or ill,
Seing they proceed from rustick Martius quill; 10
Yet how I striue to please my still pleasde freinde,
Let my true harty thoughts my lines commende:

   Bould and too bould.

To tye my thoughtes to smoth fast flatterie
Were for to scourge with whipps poore Innocence
And yf my penne should not explaine my dutie 15

---
[1] MS. And the *crossed out*.

I might be blamed much of necligence
    Speake trembling Innocence and speak the truth,
    That Honestie ingrafted in thy youth;

As A ritch Iewell of esteemed prize
That almost all men thinke Invaluable,   20
Adds comfort to the poore mans gazing eyes,
And to himself is thought inestimable
    But being lost, death is not counted cruell
    [1] To perce his hart seing he hath lost his Iewell.

Yf naked need oppressions chieffest freind,   25
With want did touch this poore sad harted soule;
His Iewell was his pawne; and in the end,
Redeemd him from proud envies fond controule,
    Then found againe tenne times his greef before
    With ioye is now redoubled, more and more;   30

I lost my Iewell then I sate me downe,
Vnder the fatall yewe and hoples pine,
One whose greene leaue the sunne did alwaies froune,
As scorning on that mournefull place to shine,   34
    With eyes orecome with teares and hart with sorrow
    The black cloked Syppres [2] sisters aid did borrow.

My Inke waxt pale, to se my face looke pale,   [fol. 48ᵇ]
My penne being pluckt from A black ravens wing,
Would wright no Sonnetts but Vlisses tale,
And of his tenne yeares absence for to sing,   40
    Tenne weekes to my sad lingring miserie,
    Were more then tenne yeares to Penellope.

---

[1] *This line is added at the side by the same hand.*
[2] *Through the trimming of the bottom of this page only the tops of S and pp remain and y has been entirely lost.*

Then how I ioy at theese weekes happie ending,
Let my forepassed greef at full relate,
How pleasure in my brest the time is spending 45
That whilome liude Alone disconsolate,
  ffound is my Iewell; Iewell vnto manie,
  More pretious in our hartes by farr then anie;

Welcome thow great Armado, frought with treasure,
Vnto the port of thy desired rest; 50
Our longing thoughts wisht for thee out of measure
As in thy Anchorage delighting best,
  Thy bodie is our barke thy hands our ores,
  To guide vs from ship ruinating shores;

Thy feete our sterne, thine eies our Admirall 55
That like A lanthorne leads vs to the baie,
Thy head our compasse that we steare with all,
Thy hart our Indean treasure and our ioy,
  Thy words our thundring Cannon that doth teare
  Our foemens ramperd walls, walles full of feare, 60

  Sailes, maste, and tacklinge, all are comprehended.
  With in thy self that hast vs still befrended;
ffor if thow hoist thy proud sailes in the wind
Blowne forth with honors resolucion
They strike their maine topp & to the Assigne 65
The chieffest place of commendacion

  ffor yf the Lyon rore by sea or land
  The craftie forrest beasts Amazd will stand
Long liue thow milkwhight terror to thy ffoes
With the great Lyones of Brytania 70
Whose verie name her foemen overthrowes
As subiugate to royall Anglia:

Deare in her sight be thow, and in o*ur* eyes,
As deare be thow to vs as dearnes lies
And to knitt vp my thoughts lest I shold rome   75
To me deare Lyon tenne times welcome home

   Yours in all duty : etc.

    R Chest [1]

XVIII.   [fol. 49ª]

Mors certa, incerta dies, incertior hora!

My prime of youth, is but a frost of cares
My feast of Ioye, is but a dish of paine
My croppe of corne, is but a field of tares
And all my goods, is but vaine hope of gaine
  The day is fled, and yet I sawe noe sunne   5
  And now I liue, & yet my liefe is dunne

The Spring is past, & yet I haue not sprung
The trees are dead, and yet my leaues be greene
My youth is past, & yet I am but yonge,
I was in world, & yet I was not seene   10
  My thried is cate,[2] and yet it is not spunne
  And now I liue, and yet my liffe is dunne

I sought for death, and found it in the wombe
I lookt for liffe, and knew it was a shade
I trod the earth, and knew it was my tombe   15
And now I die and now I was but made
  The glasse is full, and now the glasse is runne
  And now I liue and now my liffe is donne

    Finis q^d :

---

[1] Signature half trimmed away. Only the tops of letters remain.
[2] MS. ? cale.

These verses were composed by Chidiock Tichborne, who was executed in 1586 for complicity in the Babington plot. Numerous manuscript copies of this poem exist: MSS. Harl. 36, fol. 269ᵇ; 6910, fol. 141ᵇ; Sloane 3769, fol. 1ᵇ; Lansdowne 777, fol. 66ᵇ; Egerton 923, fol. 56ᵇ; B. M. Addit. 30076, fol. 27ᵇ; 30982, fol. 24 and 160; Ashmol. 781, fol. 138. This piece was first printed, as Mr. Percy Simpson kindly informs me, in a tract which appeared at the time of the execution: see Huth's *Fugitive Poetical Tracts*, First Series, No. 26. Before the end of the sixteenth century it was printed again, in John Mundy's *Songs and Psalms* (1594). The first two stanzas were included in Richard Alison's collection, *An Hour's Recreation in Music* (1606), from which they have been reprinted in Arber's *English Garner*, vi (1883), 394, and Bullen's *Shorter Elizabethan Poems*, p. 266. The full text of the piece appeared in *Reliquiae Wottonianae* (1654), pp. 511-12. The fact that Sir John Salusbury's brother, Thomas, was also among the Babington conspirators gives special point to the appearance of this poem in the Salusbury MS.

XIX.

Faith needs noe foile; foiles helpe where faith doth neede
Pure white can grace it self self grace is best
What perfect is by aide wantes of perfection
for aide bewraies a want in that which needs it
and faith in words is a bare [1] affection   5
as fire which is but fire when fuell feeds it,
yet most hould words and showes true meaninges measure
then faile I of meede since words faile me
but hold my faith sweet Sainct like hidden treasure
which is more ritch vnseene then what yow see   10
Soe is my faith but gracd, thoughe none haue knowne it
yf yow to whom I owe my faith will owne it.

Finis qᵈ/

[1] MS. *corrected from* base.

XX. [fol. 77ᵇ]

Certaine Necessary obseruations For Health [1]

Jo. Salusbury   1603

Eschewe lewde lust yf thou be wise, hote spice and wines forbeare :
Fly su[r]feit, riot and excesse, and eke long sweating here.
Rawe frutes thy stomacke will annoy : beware of drinking late :
Long watching with disordred hours, will soone impaire thy state.
Impatience is noe frend to health, a fretting irefull moode :   5
Will stirre the vaines and hurt the braine, and soone infect the bloode.
Eate seldome of the salt and sower, the windy rootes eschewe :
The lemon and the coucumber will make thy stomack rewe.
The bale and bane of eies and sight is venus winde and fyre :
Oft looking downe doth hurt them much, cold water they desire.   10
To rubb, to combe, to stretch the armes, yf fasting that thou bee :
To body, head, and spleene also, are holesome things for thee.
Noone sleepes, much slouth, and sitting still, what breed they els
   but wo :
Who euer saw a slouthfull man a healthfull body shewe.
To ache, to goute, to stone, to reume, to palsey, pyles and all :   15
A lazie body by desert is subiect and most thrall.
Vse exercise then in measure and meane, yf sound thou wilt
   be still :
But after sweat beware of cold, for that will breede much ill.
Ware how thou sit or lie on ground, for that thy ioynts will lame :
The body drawes soone from the earth, that will corupt the same.
The early morning mountaine walkes, and eke the runing streames :
Refresh the wearied spirits of man, when Phebus shews his beames.
But ware at night when dewe is fallen, and sunne by course is set :
The noysome ayre ere thou beware, will soone thy corps infect.
Apo[t]hecaries shop of drugges let not thy stomack be :   25

[1] A printed copy of this piece is bound up in Christ Church MS. 183 (fol. 4ᵃ).

Nor vse noe phisick till thou neede, thy frende aduiseth thee.
Let seldome blood but when disease, or plurisies doo call :
But after fiftie yeares be past, ware bleed thou not at all
Obserue these rules and lessons well, keep neck and feete from cold :
So mayst thou liue by natures course, till yeares haue made thee old.

XXI.

Sweet mvses come & lend your helpinge handes [fol. 82]
    to Rule my penne which quakinge standes to write
ffeare bides me stay but hope doth egge me on
    to putt in practize what's my hartes delight
ffayne would I write so 'twere without offence   5
    I'le venter once my mvse goe packe thee hence

Goe blasse abrod the prid of Britance soyle
    for vertue manhood and for curtesie
The onely perle which all prowd wale doth foyle
    for kindly favour and sobrietie   10
Kind vnto all both high & lowe degree
    to Riche & poore is worthy S a l u s b u r y

Beloued of all and Ioyed of each wight
    feared of his foes & loued of his friendes
Courteous of speech & show to all mens sight   15
    free of his purse, the flowre of all his kine
Wher e're I goe whiles lif doth last in me
    my tonge shall speake of courteus S a l u s b u r y

Did Troy but stand which nowe lyes ruinate
    & beauteus helen liueinge in the same   20
Should paris thinke with face so feminate
    or smooth tounge wordes to wynne that grekish dame
No 'twere in vayne to enterprise that deed
    since S a l u s b u r y lives that paris doth exceed.

Was paris beautifull? why so is S a l u s b u r y,
    was paris courteus? S a l u s b u r y is more kind
Was paris manlike? & is not S a l u s b u r y
    the manlikest wight in Britaine you can find
In all respectes paris vnlike to thee
    Helen revives to love sweete S a l u s b u r y

Yf S a l u s b u r y did enioye faire Helens love
    & had her salf within the wales of troy
The greekes were best their siege for to remoove
    for 'twere in vayne gainst S a l u s b u r y to enioy
His manlike armes ffrom of the greekish wales
    would tosse downe pilleres like to tennis bales

Blest be the pappes that first did give him sucke
    blest be the wombe that first did him conceyve
Blest be the tyme his father had such looke
    blest be the tree which sprwnge forth[1] such a lefe
Blest be they all & tenne tymes blest be he
    for whome so meny blessinges vtred be

Curst may they be that S a l u s b u r y seekes to wronge
    curst may they be that S a l u s b u r y seekes to shame
Curst may they be that with their slanderous tounge
    seekes to slander sweete J o h n S a l u s b u r y s name
Curst be they all & tenne tymes curst be he
    that speakes one worde against sweete S a l u s b u r y

Hence mvste I goe but mvses stay you heare
    I mvst departe yet shew you my goodwill
When I ame gon see that you doe not feare
    to shew your masteres fruites of simple skill
ffor while he lives where e're he goe or ride
    sweete J o h n S a l u s b u r y s name shall in him bide

---

[1] MS. fouth.

Denbighe adew pray thou for Salusbury [fol. 82ᵇ]
    north wales adew pray ye for Salusbury 56
The sweetest gemme that cures yo*ur* melencolie
    is kind & faire & courteus Salusbury
Pray you for him & I will pray for yee
    so god blesse vs & courteus Salusbury 60

Nowe mvses stay I may no longer write
    to dolle[1] ame I to speake of Salusbury prais
Some finer wittes hearafter shall indite
    & putt his name in coridons roondelays
Then sweete philida & coridon agree 65
    to singe in prays of lovinge Salusbury

And I'le intreat dianas trayne to stand
    to lend ye help w*i*th all their siluer stringes
The nimphes shall dance w*i*th Salusbury hand in hand
    treadinge the measures on the pleasant plaines 70
And thus in myddest of all his mirth & glee
    I'le take my leaue of courteus Salusbury
        finis quoth Danielle.

XXII.

But stay a while thou hast forgott thy parte [fol. 83ᵃ]
    retourne againe & ere thou goe ffrom hence
Thinke vpon her whome thou arte bou*n*d in harte
    in humble duty for to recompence
ffor whom he loves shee neuer hates I see 5
    so kind & courteus is m[istress] Salusbury

ffrom princely blood & Ryale stocke she came
    of egles brood hatcht in a loftie nest
The earle of derby & the kinge of manne
    her father was her brother now possest 10
Then hapie he but thris more hapie's shee
    to mache her self w*i*th lovely Salusbury

---

[1] MS. *A letter has been deleted after* d.

A lovelier man all europe cannot find
    so kind to her & she so kind to him
Like turtles true so doth this cuple buyld   15
    heauens graunte this their ioyes may ne're be dime
But flwrish still as doth the lawrel tree
    & hartes content rest both to him & shee

Nowe mvst I goe my penne hath runne his fill
    gould have I not to gwrder[1] her with all   20
But yet to shew some parte of my good will
    the best I have I humblie parte with all
Accept it then a portion of my store
    'tis my good will would god 'twere tenne tymes more

Thus for my bowldnes pardon I do crave   25
    prayeinge the heauens to send you both content
Ioy of your ofspringe euer for to have
    Admetus lif vnto you both be lent
God keepe your troope both high & lowe degree
    tho last not lest vale m[istress] Ane stanley   30
        finis quoth Danielle

XXIII.

In Motto Mecænatis.   [fol. 83ᵇ]

Posse et Nolle Nobile.

A worthie man deserues a worthie Motte,
As badge therby his Nature to declare.
Wherfore the fates, of purpose did alotte,
to this braue Squire, this Symbole sweet & rare.:
Of Might to spoyle, but yett of Mercie spare.   5
A Symbole sure to Salsberie due by right :
whose still doth ioyne, his Mercie with his Might.

[1] ? guerdon.

Thoughe Lyonlike, his P o s s e might take place,
yett like a lambe he N o l l e vseth aye;
Right like himself (the floure of S a l s b e r i e s race) 10
who neuer as yett a poore man woulde dismaye;
but princockes pryde, he vsd to daunt allwaye,
And so doth still: wherby is knowne full well,
His Noble mynde, and Manhood to excell.

All crauen curres y^t comes of castrell kynde, 15
are knowne full well; when they thier might woulde strayne
The poore t'oppresse, that woulde their fauoure fynde,
or yelde himself, their ffrendshippe to attayne.
Then, seruile sottes triumphes in might amayne
But such as comes from Noble Lyons race, 20
(like this braue Squire) who yeeldes, recyues to grace.
      Haud ficta loquor. Hughe Gryphyth.

  This poem was printed in 1597 by Robert Parry in his *Sinetes Passions*, from which it was reprinted by Dr. Grosart in his Introduction to Chester's *Love's Martyr*, p. xvi. In a document dated March 17 in the forty-fifth year of Elizabeth, Hugh Gruffith appears as the holder of land at Wrexham (*Archaeol. Cambrensis*, Suppl. vol. i, Original Doc., p. ccclii). The same name occurs also among the tenants of Marchwiail (i.e. Ruabon)—ibid., pp. cxciv–cxcv.

XXIV.

J. S. his amasement.

Griefe is the sea that ouerflowes my hart,   [fol. 84]
Droun'de by my thoughts, that doe procure my smart,
My thoughts, and griefes be waywarde Dearest Deare,
Because I misse thee, when I wish thee neare/
And that I rest yppon thy auntient Loue, 5
Which chainge of time, nor absense cannot moue,
But all thy thoughts of me (I feare) are flowne,
Because thow think'st I holde thee not mine owne/
Or else thy hart, and thoughts, wolde breake with paine,

To think vppon the griefe that I sustaine/ 10
Being such, as bearing in my trobled brest.
Olde auntient Loue : Nue griefes will neuer rest.
For thee my trust, my Life, my hart, my restles ioy
Is knowne, is pawn'd, is trobled with annoy.
Compare the cause of my much strainge estate/ 15
And thow wil'te thinke I am vnfortunate.
And yt wolde make thy womanish breast to bleede,
With sobbs of sorowe, from fowle griefe not freede,
Which I in honest Loue will rather hide,
Then thow for me impatience sholdst abide/ 20
And still be hardly thought of, and endure
Such plurall death of minde, which you procure/
Rather then you shall once your finger moue,
Or cause to ake : I will conceale my Loue :
Vntill the time my thoughts, and cares be free/ 25
I cannot rest (my Sweet) but thinke on thee/
I wolde not wish my griefe (my Loue) be knowne,
Nor in the popular opemouth'de worlde be blowne/
That is the cause that makes my cariadge strainge
To thee thow think'st : and yet mine eye doth rainge 30
Sparcling out Loue fires, on thy Lillie brest
Wheare PHILVMELA builds her softe-down'de nest.
That auntient Loue to thee I haue profest.
Makes thee to thinke I hate thee with the rest.
Thoughe still I dote : and wolde not haue thee knowe yt 35
Till time, and place, doe serue for me to showe yt,
My head, my hart, mine eyes, my Lippes, my tounge,
Shall medytate thy praise, and singe a songe,
Of neuer dyinge Loue : set to the Lute
By great APOLLO, making VENVS mute, 40
As blussing, for to heare thy bewties glorrie,
And vertues to bedecke my happy storye ;
Sleeping, or waking, going, or sittinge still,
Seeing, hearing, tasting, feeling, speaking, shall fulfill,
And with this Concordant Pilgrim must agree 45

Vntill the time that thoughts and I be free
All dismall death, all plunging plagues, all greeuous grones,
All gulphes of griefe, all woes, and piteous mones,
All anguish, and what else procureth paine   [fol. 84ᵇ]
For thee I feele, and euer shall sustaine   50
All pleasures, pastimes, mirth, and luckye ioyes
All happy howres, and euer blessed daies,
Are gone, are fled, are vaded and are spente,
Vnlesse thy Crimson-colored hart relent;
And that my happes, my future hopes fulfill,   55
My hopes by happes mischaunce my hart will kill.
Soe hopes, and happes, and all shalbe deceaued,
Vnlesse by thee my sweete they be releaued./

         Τελως   J. S.

XXV.

I fauste Herculeo counctos qui robore præstas,   [fol. 86ᵇ]
O ptime flos patriæ, vinces virtute coævos.
A nte oculos Domini semper timor esto tonantis.
N obile pectus habes, magnorum dignus avorum,
N on prece, nec pretio tua mens corumpitur vllo.   5
E sto viris tutela bonis, et sontibus horror,
S olamen miseris, sis mite levamen egenis.
S ospitet in patriæ dulcis te commoda christus.
A scanius proceres inter ceu splendidus extas,
L una velut stellas excellens luce minores.   10
V tere consilijs præbere senilibus aures,
S ic tibi continget rerum pax læta tuarum.
B elle nunc mores collustrat candor avitus.
V ive diu spes ac certissima cura tuorum
R arum quem sentit vicinia tota patronum.   15
I nnocuus longum traduc feliciter ævum.
V rsula fælices, hæroica fæmina, coniux
S alua Sybillenos cum nato compleat annos

                finis   Bernardus Iones, 1596.

XXVI.

D elite doth nessell in her comelie face [fol. 87]
O n heade or heare like radiant Phebus strange
R adiant eies that light the darkest place
O heavenlie eies such heare Evaddna twynes
T wo Cheris fel in beaten swgwr white 5
H er cheekes of them the coller do reserve [1]
I n her sweete lippes; the taste of them are sweete
E ternall praise, fayer Cheekes sweet lippes deserve

H er naked necke as white as silver swanne
A s silver swanne or rarest lilie flowre 10
L et silver byrd or lily flower wax wan
S uch white is hers as ever shall endure
A ppelles payntinge venus face and breaste
L efte the other partes impolisd [sic ?] without arte
L ord all the world canot expresse the rest 15
  of this sweete wighte sole solace of my harte

finis   J. S.

XXVII.

[fol. 87^b]

This Poysie was presented In A Maske att Berine In Christmas the xxvijth oF Desember 1586 : vnto M^{ris} Katherin Thelloall, Beinge written In A Sheelde And Deliuerede by William Winne OF LLanver Esquier at the Mariage of Iohn Salisburye of LLeweny Esquier Her Sonne and heaire wth Vrsula Stanley Daughter vnto the righte Honorable Henrie Earle of Derbye And devisede by Roger Salisburye of bachegerige Esquier

> Dame Venus deare youe Maye Rejoyce
> at your Sonne Cupides happye Choyse
> To hym as By the Gods Asseignde 10
> For to delighte hys doulfull mynde &c.

The ninth line was first written at this point and afterwards crossed out.

This other Poysie was pʳsentede in The former Maske in A Sheelde alsoe by Rog: Sal: of bach: esquier Vnto Vr: Sal: wyfe Vnto Mʳ Io: Sa: Afore saide And devised by the sayde Rog: Sal:

> The Lyon Rampinge for his Praye
> A princlye byrde hee dyd Assaye
> and hauinge winges to flye at Will,
> yet Caughte her faste & houlds hir still
> Wᵗʰ hyr to sporte as Lyckes them beste,
> Thoughe Lions stoute vse not to jest
> A thinge moste strange yet is ytt trewe,
> God graunt them Joy and so Adewe.
>
>   Finies Vrsula Salisburye
>
>   1592.

XXVIII.

D ames diamond: dame beautyes darling deare   [fol. 88ᵃ]
O nix of hono*ur*: voide of staynes deface
R uby enrichd: wⁱth favours comely cheare
O fspring of ould: renowmed nobele race
T ype in thy tyme: of¹ virtue gifftes and grace
H igh helicon: thy walke beseemeth well
Y eald nymphes your seate: goe otherwhere to dwell

H ymene hath: handfasted wedlocks knott
A don to thee: mad scape from venus Lapp
L ykyng hath ledd: thy hand to drawe thy lott
S yth hymene: hath handed thee thy happ
A nd adon eke: portrayed lykinges mapp
L ynke harte to hand: and love to Like knytt fast
L ive Long to Love: and Love while Lyf doth last
   What goodwill frames no goodwill blames.
  finis

      [Signature obliterated by pen marks.]

   MS. verte *crossed out.*

XXIX. [fol. 88ᵇ]

Dayne not to love where love ys freelye lent
Or yf goodwill by love be truly ment
Refuce not love that will not soone relent
Once lovd in hart will love and be content
Therby thy love maye grace thy sex and kynd 5
How that a woman beares a lovinge[1] mynd
Yeld then to love and love be sure to fynd

Helena fayre and lucrece chast of cheare
Adoreth thee and seemely service sweare
Lavinia and penelope do heare 10
Suich fame of thee that they thy presens feare
And adon eke thy love and coupled make
Left venus bowre for thy sweete beautyes sake
Like love and live and so my leave I take.

    no want of will but want of skyll 15
    what love deviseth no love dyspyseth

     finis : Jo Salusburye 1593.

XXX.

In obitum Catharinæ Tudir [fol. 174]
  Epitaphium.

Hic defuncta iacet Catharina, britannica Phœnix,
 quam rapuit Celeri, mors inopina manu.
Hæc fuit egregij proles generosa Tuderi,
 quondam Roberto neptis amata suo.
Non opus, antiquos proavos extollere, cuncti 5
 agnoscunt generis stemmata clara sui.
Quattuor illa viris, vinclo connexa iugali,
 traduxit vitam laude, et honore piam.

---

[1] *Interlined above* constant *crossed out.*

E quibus illa trium, Crudelia fata gemebat,
  illius at quarto mors dolet atra viro. 10
Horum de primis floret generosa propago,
  quam Christus dextra protegat ille sua.
Salsburius reliquos inter supereminet omnes,
  spes gentis, summus quem regat ipse deus.
Illa peragravit multas tutissima terras, 15
  secura in medijs fluctibus illa fuit.
Nam protector eras illi venerande Iehova,
  permansit solo numine tuta tuo.
Vixit sex decies, si demas quattuor annos,
  dormijt in domino tunc Catharina deo. 20
Languida mortifero repleta Berennia luctu, [fol. 174ᵇ]
  deplorat dominæ tristia fata suæ.
Splendida lugubres patitur Lawenia [1] planctus,
  heu quantos fletus angulus omnis habet,
Maynan amena dolet, Melai gemit, utque Bachegraig, 25
  tristia sunt istis pectora multa locis.
Splendida consimiles sensit Gwederia luctus,
  denique Plaswardi regia tecta dolet.
Edwardus vitam ducit Theloallus amaram,
  amisit sponsam (res miseranda) suam. 30
Luctisono tristes resident in corde dolores,
  quales ex animo sæcula nulla trahent.
Tota dolorificum perpessa est Rossia luctum,
  vnius ob mortem pectora mille gemunt.
Cum genitore puer flet, cum genitrice puella, 35
  neptis cum vetula, cum vetuloque nepos.
Sponsaque cum sponso patitur gemebunda dolorem,
  cumque nuru socrus, cum generoque socer.
Et ne prolixus longis ambagibus vtar,
  præ fletu madidas omnibus ecce genas. 40
Sed quid Conducunt lachrimæ, suspiria, planctus?
  aspera non lachrimæ flectere fata valent.

---

[1] I. e. Lleweni.

Hæc est nimirum mortalibus orbita Cunctis,
    vt Caro pulvis erat, sic caro pulvis erit.
Sed tamen ista caro, de pulvere viva resurget,   45
    tunc erit æterno consociata deo.
Iam Catharina vale, summo dilecta Iehovæ,
    grataque Cælicolis, o Catharina, vale.

                    per me Owenum Jones, Clericum.[1]

XXXI.

Dialogus   [fol. 175]

Argumentum dialogi.
Omnis Catrinam populus deplorat ademptam.
Sic author populi luctum Cohibere laborat.

Interlocutores populus et author.

Populus. O gemebunda dies ævo tristissima nostro,   5
    o mala męstitiæ tempora plena feræ.
Terribiles o quam nescitis parcere Parcæ ?
    quantaque sunt nostris gaudia vestra malis ?

Eighty-six lines in all, concluding :
                                            [fol. 176]
Populus. Sic faciam ; summusque pater mea verba benigne
    excipiat : dic tu Candide lector. amen.   10

            per eundem Owenum Jones Clericum.

[1] Owen Jones appears again in several Welsh MSS. in the Brit. Museum : Addit. 14964, 14965 (end), and 15056.

XXXII.

[fol. 177]

In obitum illustrissimæ dominæ Catharinæ Tudir Berennensis carmen lugubre, quæ obijt mortem xxvij die Augusti anno do : 1591.

Heu modo musa veni, lugubria dicere fata,
  mixtaque sit lachrimis nænia męsta tuis.
Claræ ploremus Catharinæ funera Cuncti,
  quam nobis triplices eripuere deæ.

One hundred and eight lines in all, concluding:

Molliter ossa, precor, recubent sub marmore tecta, [fol. 178ᵇ]
  tu tamen elysijs ipsa quiesce. Vale.

Dauid Jones.

XXXIII.

[fol. 179]

The Epitath of mistris Katheryn Theloall whoe deceased the xxviith day of Auguste and was buried the first of September folowinge in the yeare of our lord god 1591.

The blustringe blastes of sturdie storme, wyth duskie vapore
                Covers,
    the welkyn aye in rackinge Cloudes, the boysterous
                Boreas hovers.
Triton beinge wett wyth raging waves the mightie whall
                doyth stride,
    to saue hymself from Neptunes wrath in ffrothye waters
                glide.

Ninety-two lines in all, concluding:

[fol. 180ᵇ]

And then no doubt in tyme you shall, wyth her in heaven
                appeere   5
    for to enioye her Companie, as earst you haue donne
                heere.

finis,   Robert Parry   gentleman.

XXXIV.

An Epitath made one the deathe of mistries Katheryn Theloall by Cadwaladr Wynn gent.[1]

Seinge god eche lyvinge thinge on earthe, from tyme to tyme here sendes,
   which hence in tyme wearinge away, but for a tyme he lendes.

Thirty-two lines in all, concluding:

[fol. 181]

(To ende this worldly trace) her happe was, Theloall laste to have
   and then her daughter had by Wynn, vnto his heire she gave.

finis.

Cadwalader Wynn of Voylas held the office of sheriff in the County of Denbigh in 1605.—See *Hist. MSS. Com.*, Report on Welsh MSS., i (1899), p. 799; also Edward Parry, *List of High Sheriffs of the Co. of Denbigh*, Denbigh, 1906.

XXXV.

A sorowfull complainte or Epitaphe vpon the deathe of the worshipfull Katheryn Theloall daughter and heyre to Tyder ap Robert Esq. whoe deceased the xxvij[th] *day of Auguste, and was enterred the first of September folowinge, in the yeare of our lorde god 1591, by Robert Salusbury Esq.*[2] *Doctor of the civille Lawe.*

As sacred sisters twayne, mans lyne doyth twist and drawe,
   soe doythe the third abridge the same, without Controll or awe.

[1] *Another hand has crossed out* gent *and written :* of Vŏylas Esquier.
[2] *This word crossed out.*

Seventy lines in all, concluding:

[fol. 182]

Wyth our redeemer Christ, whoe graunt vs all his heavenly grace
that flittinge hence, in blisse wyth hym, for ever we may haue place.

finis.

Doctor Robert Salusbury was an uncle of our Sir John Salusbury; he married Margaret daughter to Edward Stanley (see Dwnn's *Heraldic Visit. of Wales*, Ed. Samuel R. Meyrick, Welsh MSS. Soc. Llandovery, 1846, ii. 331). I am not certain whether he was the same as Sir Robert Salusbury Knt., Sheriff of the County of Denbigh in 1597 (*Hist. MSS. Com.*, Report on Welsh MSS., i, p. 799), who died June 5, 1601 (*Hist. MSS. Com.*, Report XI, App. Part VII, p. 146).

Poems

by

Sir John Salusbury

INCLUDED IN A SMALL VOLUME DEDICATED TO HIM BY
'ROBERT PARRY, GENT.' PRINTED IN 1597, OF
WHICH THE UNIQUE COPY IS PRESERVED IN THE
LIBRARY OF S. R. CHRISTIE-MILLER, ESQ^{re},
AT BRITWELL COURT.

THE

Patrone his pa-
thetical Posies,
Sonets, Maddri-
galls, & Rown-
delayes.

Together

With Sinetes

Dompe

Plena verecun | di culpa pu | doris erat.

POESIE I.

[D. 7 recto]

The patrones conceyte:

D omesticke Goddes of the Sea-whal'd Isle,
Heau'ns erected trophies of thy prayes,
Avroras blush, that beautifies thy smile,
Shines far more bright then Phœbus goulden rayes,
  Natures chiefe pride, the map of beauties grace,   5
  Loues louely sweete, which vertue doth embrace.

O f-spring of fludds, borne of the salt-sea foame,
Thoughts-maze that doth to Pallas bower inclines
A Commet, that in starrie night doth gloame.
And doth presage of misteries diuine?   10
  An ornament, bedeck'd with goulden tyres,
  A pearle in camp'd in strength of chaste desires.

R eposed rest of Adon's ardent looke.
Thy Christall-pointed eies (like Saphyres blue,
Set in the snowe) doe hide a bayted hooke :   15
Which doth intrap by force of Goulden hue :
  Were Adon here to viewe thy Venvs eye
  Could Adon such a Venvs suite denye.

O lympus Queene, that doth commaunde the skyes,
Whose shining beam's doe light the westerne Isle,   20
No base aspect in thy sweete bodie lies,
Thy fauours doe the stealing time beguile :
  For precious breath so doth perfume the ayre,
  That all applaude thou onl art sweete and faire.

T he Radian beam's of natur's purest die,   [D. 7 verso]
With honours Equipage long liue thy fame,   26
Whose siluer arkes, surpassing Christall skie,

Doth force loue Queene to reuerence thy name :
    Starrs doe inuay, that earth retaineth thee,
    From making Fourth amongst the graces Three.   30

H eau'ns newe ioy, earth's possessed wonder,
The welkins pride,[1] if they might thee embraece,
As they did IOVES loue that kills with thunder,
Thy memorie her beautie doth deface.
    Liue long thou star, which in the North doth shine, 35
    That noble worth's may fill thy sacred shrine.

Y mpe graft with vertue in her tender yeeres,
Deriuing honour from her noble stocke,
Which Needles weare ? for honour still appeer's
Within her browe, which doth fames cradle rocke ;   40
    Whose searching wit, dipt in MINERVAS vaine,
    Fraught with content, doth Pallas prayses staine.

H IBBLA hath Bees, stor'd with a sweete encrease,
A nd shee hath beautie, furnished with grace,
L iue stinges doe pricke, though hony's taste to please, 45
S o woundes her beautie those which it embrace :
    A Lampe of glorie shines in thee alone,
    L iue long in earth thou match-lesse Paragone.

POSIE II.   [D. 8 recto]

The Patrone's affection.

L aunterne of loue the patrone due of lore,
L ight some beame my affection to guide,
A mongst the drerie throbbes encreasing sore,
S ore in the vaile of heart where I them hide :
L anguishing in delight I doe delight to pine   5

---

[1] *Printed* ptide.

A nd can I pine a more contented paine,
H art once mine-owne, is nowe possession thine,
Y eilde then to yeilde this hearts due entertaine.
H onour is the guest, let bounty be my prize,
T ruth be the page of my admired light, 10
O ccasion be thou prest at my aduize,
R egarding hand, and hart, t'attend her sight.
    O r else my heart and minde I hould in hand :
      D oe then my hope confirme that hope may stand.

Posie III.

The patrones phantasie.

T ormented heart in thrall,   **Y** ea thrall to loue,
R especting will,   **H** eart-breaking gaine doth grow,
E uer Dolobelia,   **T** ime so will proue,
B inding distresse,   **O** gem wilt thou allowe,
T his fortune my will   **R** epose-lesse of ease,   5
V nlesse thou Leda,   **O** uer-spread my heart,
C utting all my ruth, dayne   **D** isdaine to cease,
I yeilde to fate, and welcome endles   **S** mart.

Posie IIII.   [D. 8 verso]

The Patrons pauze in ode.

D impl's florish, beauties grace,
F ortune smileth in thy face,
E ye bewrayeth honours flower,
L oue is norish'd in thy bower,
I n thy bended brow doth lye, 5
Z eale imprest with chastitie.
    I oue's darling deere,

O pale lippes of corall hue,
R arer die then cheries newe,
A rkes where reason cannot trie, 10
B eauties riches which doth lye,
E ntomb'd in that fayrest frame,
T ouch of breath perfumes[1] the same.
    O rubie cleere.

R ipe ADON fled VENVS bower, 15
A yming at thy sweetest flower,
H is ardent loue forst the same,
W onted agents of his flame :
O rbe to whose enflamed fier,
L oue incens'd him to aspire. 20
    H ope of our time,

O riad's of the hills drawe neere,
N ayad's come before your peere :
F lower of nature shining shoes,
R iper then the falling rose, [E. 1 recto]
E ntermingled with white flower, 26
S tayn'd with vermilion's power.
    N estl'd in our clime.

T he siluer swans sing in poe,
S ilent notes of newe-spronge woe, 30
T uned notes of cares I sing,
O rgan of the muses springe,
N atures pride inforceth me,
E u'n to rue my destinie.
    S tarre shew thy might, 35

H elens beautie is defac'd,
I o's graces are disgrac'd,
R eaching not the twentith part,
O f thy gloases true desart,

---

[1] *Printed* petfumes.

But no maruaile thou alone, 40
E u'n art VENYS paragone,
　　Arm'd with delight.

Iris coulors are to base,
She would make APELLES gaze,
Resting by the siluer streame, 45
Tossing nature seame by seame,
Pointing at the Christall skie,
Arguing her maiestie,
　　Loues rampire stronge　　　　[E. 1 verso]

Hayre of Amber, fresh of hue, 50
Wau'd with goulden wyers newe,
Riches of the finest mould,
Rarest glorie to behould,
Pmpe with natures vertue graft,
Engines newe for dolors fraught 55
　　Eu'n there are spronge,

A Iem fram'd with Diamounds,
In whose voice true concord sounds,
Ioy to all that ken thy smile,
In thee doth vertue fame beguile, 60
In whose beautie burneth fier,
Which disgraceth Queene desier:
　　Saunce all compare,

Loue it selfe being brought to gaze,
Learnes to treade the louers maze; 65
Lying vncou'red in thy looke,
Left for to vnclaspe the Booke:
Where enroul'd thy fame remaines,[1]
That IVNOS blush of glory staines:
　　Blot out my care. 70

[1] *Printed* remaiues.

S pheare containing all in all,
O nely fram'd to make men thrall :
Onix deck'd with honours worth,
On whose beautie bringeth foorth :   [E. 2 recto]
Smiles ou'r clouded with disdaine,   75
Which loyall heart doth paine :
    V oyde of disgrace,

A VRORA's blush that decks thy smile,
W ayting louers to beguile :[1]
Where curious thoughts built the nest,   80
Which neu'r yeildes to louers rest :
Wasting still the yeilding eye,
Whilst he doth the beautie spie
    R ea'd in her face.

L ampe enric'hd with honours flower,   85
B lossome gracing VENVS bower :
Bearing plumes of feathers white,
Wherein Turtles[2] doe delighte,
Sense would seme to weake to finde,
Reason's depth in modest minde :   90
    Y eilding desire.

L ode-starre of my happie choyse,
I n thee alone I doe reioyce :
O happie man whose hap is such,
To be made happie by thy tutch :   95
Thy worth and worthynes could moue
The stoutest to incline to loue,
    E nflam'd with fier.

[1] *Printed* begnile.
[2] *Printed* Tnrtles.

Posie V. [E. 2 verso]

The dittie to Sospiros.

The wound of hart doth cause my sighes to spring
And sighes doe oft report my hartie sore,
This sore of heart doth woefull tidings bring,
That loue is lacke and I doe grieue therefore :
    O sighes why doe you rise and take no rest,   5
    O heart why art thou thus with them possest.

My heart in selfe it selfe would pine away,
if that sometimes sighes musicke I shoulde misse,
This bitter ioy and pleasant paine must staie,
The greatest griefe is now my greatest blisse :   10
    The night I grone the day I teare my heart,
    I loue these sighes I triumph in their smart.

When minde and thought are clogged with their cares
And that my heart is readie for to breake,
Then eu'rie sigh doth question how it fares,   15
And heart to them replies that it is weake.
    [1][Th]er after sighes the heart is some-what glad,
    [Th]us without sower the sweete is neuer had.

My wish and will for succour doe aspire,   [E. 3 recto]
Vnto the seate of my endeered trust,   20
But want and woe ensuing my desire,
My heart doth quaile and after sigh it must :
    Yet wish I must and well I may delight,
    Though sighe for wants and woes doe me affright.

These sighes Ile entertaine[2] though they me noy,   25
For they doe like the cause from where they rise,

---
[1] *Corner of page torn.*
[2] *Printed* entertertaine.

They bring in port newes of my mynded ioy,
And as they passe they message me no lies:
    And yet they leaue behinde them such a want,
    That minde and ioy I finde to be but scant,   30

O will you neuer cease me sighes to grieue,
And maye not hope keepe you in calme repose,
Let me some respite haue, hart to relieue,
Lest that your selues and you fullie lose:
    Sighes doe aspire till they obtaine their will,   35
    Sighes will not cease they seeke my heart to kill.

POSIE 6.   [E. 3 verso]

The patrones Dilemma.

Of stately stones the **D**iamond is kinge,
Whose splendor doth dazell the gazing eye,
The **O**nix gloze, is tyed to honors winge,
Whose vertu's gouern'd by th'imperiall skie:
    These graces all in thee combin'd remaine,   5
    For glorie thine their glories still doth staine.

Shall I not speake of **R**ubies glorious blaze,
That I blazeth still, like blazing star that shoes,
Or cease to write how men at th'**O**pale gaze,
Whose beautie shines like perles of dewe on rose: 10
    These vertues all (compar'd with thine) are base,
    For nature gaue thee excellent of grace.

The **T**opas chast thou doest in kind excell,
The **H**yacinth that strangers loue procures,
Hath not such force, nor can not worke so well,   15
As honors beautie still in thee alures;
    Yris shews not more coulors in her kind,
    Then vertues be with in thy noble mind.

The windie **H**istmos shews, and bright aspects, [E. 4 recto]
Comes far behind this faire **A**ngragos worth, 20
The **L**upinar hath not more chast affects.
Then glorie of th'vnspotted minde brings foorth.
    My paines encrease thy graces to repeate,
    For cold despaire driues out of hope the heate.

Yf **S**aunus fort which doth expell deceate, 25
Or **A**gathes which happie bouldnes yeild's,
And eke **L**uperius whose vertues greate,
Doth glad the minde : all which are found in feilds :
    Yf these I had to comfort my despaire,
    Hope yet might hope to win & weare thy faire. 30

POSIE. VII. [E. 4 verso]

The Palmers Dittie vppon his Almes.

Favre Dole the flower of beawties glorious shine,
Whose sweete sweet grace true guerdon doth deserue,
My Orisons I offer to thy shrine,
That beauties name in glories state preserue :
    My hap (ô haplesse hap) that gaue th'applause, 5
    Thy beautie view'd when trembling hart did pause.

Were I a King, I would resigne my Crowne,
To gaine the name of Palmers happie kinde,
I would not craue to liue in high renowne,
If Dole I had to satisfie my minde : 10
    Then I for Dole a Palmers name would craue,
    If Palmer might be sure his dole to haue.

Posie. VIII.

The Patrones Adiew.

Y f loue deserues the fruit of loues desire,
H ope loathes my loue to liue in hope of right:
T ime after triall once may quench my fire,
O h salue the sore and cherish my delight:
R ue lawles force, which feruent zeale procures. 5
O btaine a hart like to the Emerauld pure:
D ayne hope to graunt where feare dispaire allures,
I n deepe distresse naught but true faith is sure.

Poesie IX. [E. 5 recto]

Fides in Fortunam.

Most sacred is the sweete where fortune swayes,
Deuine the sound of her enchaunting voice.
Noe hope of rest, wher hope, true hope delayes,
Though[1] I dispaire I may not change me choise:
    For hue [sic] I well, though fortune me dispise, 5
    To honour her, that scornes my enterprise.

To bandie lookes will ease my thrauled heart,
With lookes, my life shalbe at her commaunde,
Yf so much grace to faith she will impart:
With lookes againe, to answere my demaunde; 10
    And that I may still loue her to my graue,
    With purest faith, is all that I doe craue.

Let Phœbus drawe his shining beam's away,
Let heau'ns forsake to graunt me any light,
Let foode me faile; let hope, my hope delay; 15

[1] *Printed* Thongh.

Let eares not heare ; let watch-full eies want sight :
    Let sense, my sense, with furies fell confound,
    Before that faith, to fortune false be found.

Thy eu'r sworne friende, and seruant to thy end,
Hath made a vowe and promise with his soule.[1]   20
His fortun's right with courage to defend,
Against proudest he, this offer dare controle :
    My match is sure if Fortune grace her swayne,
    And coulors giue her quarrell to maintaine.   24

Colours they are of purest Indian die,   [E. 5 verso]
For none but such doth Fortune vse to lend.
Whose sight may moue the coward neu'r to flie,
And all his force against his foe to bend.
    Then let sweet soule thy colours be my guide,
    And hap what maye, thy doome I will abide.   30

Then write thy Censure with thy prettie hand,
I will obay the sentence of thy minde,
And graue the same in table faire to stand ;
So that, ensuing age the same may finde :
    For monument in goulden letters wrought,   35
    To whet with sight the accents of my thought.

POESIE X.   [E. 6 recto]

My sorrov is ioy.

Sowre is the sweet that sorrow doth mainetaine,
Yet sorrow's good, that yeildeth mickle ioy,
True ioy he hath, that can from ioy refrayne.
Which haruest's still the fruites of deepe annoy :
    Yet I enthraulde in blind CVPIDOS snare,   5
    With fond conceyte in sorrows ioy I faire.

---

[1] *Printed* sonle.

Fortun's my ioy, which sorrow still doth yeild,
Her frowne I count a fauour to my soule ;
Sorrow doth sway, and ioy hath lost the field,
Yet fame in minde doth often ioy enro'le :   10
    But when I thinke for whom I beare this smart,
    It yeilds new ioy vnto my carefull hart.

POESIE.   XI.   [E. 6 verso]

An almon for a Parrat.

Disdainfull dames that mountaines moue in thought,
And thinke they may Ioues thunder-bolt controule,
Who past compare ech one[1] doe set at naught,
With spuemish scorn's that nowe in rethorick roule :
    Yet scorne that will be scorn'd of proude disdaine,   5
    I scorne to beare the scornes of finest braine.

Gestures, nor lookes of simpring coy conceyts,
Shall make me moue for stately ladies mocks :
Then SIRENS cease to trap with your deceyts,
Least that your barkes meete vnexpected rocks :   10
    For calmest ebbe may yeild[2] the roughest tide,
    And change of time, may change in time your pride.

Leaue to conuerse if needes you must inuay,
Let meaner sort feede on their meane entent,
And soare on still, the larke is fled awaye,   15
Some one in time will pay what you haue lent,
    Poore hungrie gnatts faile not on wormes to feede,
    When goshaukes misse on hoped pray to speede.

[1] *Printed* oue.   [2] *Printed* yelld.

POESIE. XII. [E. 7 recto]

The authors muse vpon / his Conceyte.

Faire, fairest, faire ; is passing faire, be faire,
Let not your deed's obscure your beauties faire.
The Queene so faire of Fearies not more fayer,
Which doth excell with fancies chiefest fayer,
    Fayre to the worldes faire admiring wonder,   5
    Fayrer then IOVES loue that kills with thunder.

Eu'n to your swayne you seeme prides passing faire,
That naught desires but fortun's faire to reape,
Yf fortune then will driue me to despaire,
No change can make your sweetest faire so cheape,   10
    But that I must, and will liue in exile,
    Before your thoughtes with thought I will defile.

Fayre fierce to faith, when fortune bend her browes,
Yet fortune sweete be thou reclaym'd againe :
For vnto thee I offer all my vowes,   15
That may appease the rigor of my paine :
    Yeilde wished hope after this stormie blast,
    That calm's repose may worke content at last.

POSIE. 13. [E. 7 verso]

Fides ad fortunam.

The goulden Phebus (longing oft) is seene,
To pricke his furious steedes to run in haste,
To clip and coll faire Thetis louely Queene,
In pensiue thoughts lest he the time should waste,
    So I make speede thy selfe for to embrace,   5
    Beinge almost tyr'd in pursuite of the chase.
For houndes vncoupled, range the forrest wide,
The stance being prun'd, I watch the rowsed game,

And to the marke my shaftes full well I guide :
The craftie Doo takes on then to be lame : 10
 But hauing past the daunger of my bowe,
 She, limping leaues, and hastes away to goe.
Thus I being surest of my hoped sport,
Still misse the fairest marke that eu'r was kend,
Words doe abound of comfort to exhorte, 15
But deedes are slowe sure promises to end :
 The hope then[1] left is game to rowse anewe,
 (Till deedes supplie) and feede my selfe with view.
Fortune hath sayde, and I beleeued that,
Renewed hope might ease my heart neere spent : 20
Despaire in sequel oft my hope doth squat ;
That doubtfull I remaine still discontent,
 Wherefore to faith if faith remaine in thee,
 With faithfull wordes let deedes in one agree.

FINIS.

SONETTO. I.   [E. 8 recto]

Reade these my lines the the [sic] carrecters of care,
Sweete Nymph those lynes reade ou'r & ou'r[2] againe,
View in this glasse (that glorie doth prepare,)
The depth of worthes which in thee doth remaine,
Heare I set foorth the garden of thy grace, 5
With plentie stor'd of choyse and sweetest flowers,
Where I for thee abortiue thoughtes embrace ;
When in conceyte hope lodgeth in thy bowers.
Heare shalt thou finde the Orphans of my hope,
Shad'wed with vaile en'n [sic] of thy rare deseart, 10
Of all my thoughtes here shalt thou finde the scope,
Which to the worlde thy honour shalt ympart.
 Thus will I say when skies aduaunce thy name,
 Liue HELENS peere eternized thy fame.

[1] *Printed* theu.   [2] *Printed* on'r.

Sonetto. 2. [E. 8 verso]

Farewell my hope thy hap did thee not steede,
And thou my hap vnhappie come to mee,
Farewell my trust which voide wast of all meede,
And thou heart-sore attend my miserie,
Farewell my hold which wast to stronge to hold, 5
And thou my ruine welcome to my gaine,
Farewell my life which dead are in my mould,
And life no life torment my hart with paine.
Farewell my chiefe that conquerst with thy looke,
And thraldome I appeale to riue my heart, 10
Farewell my thought, thy thought she will not brooke,
Yet thinke I will for that I feele the smart.
Farewell my choise I lastly doe thee chuse,
I cannot chuse another to my will:
Farewell my comfort comfortles o muse, 15
And sorrowe weake thy wrath my ioy to spill.
    Farewell long stay for winde to fill thy sayle,
    Come banishment. Adieû, loue must preuayle.

Sonetto. 3. [F. 1 recto]

E merald of treasure eternall spring,
N urst by the graces day-starre shine on hie,
I ngendring perfect blisse with valens ring:
T wisting loue and liking with constancie.
N ow stanchlesse hart redres & soule-sick wound, 5
E nwrap the same in foldes of fresh desire,
L et loûe be waking haruest hope be found,
A nd liuing spring to quench this flame of fier.
V nto your excellent loue sole commaund,
S eing ês you may procure I me commend, 10
I nto your counsels grace voutch my demaund,
H eate burning ioy sustaine in ioyfull end.
    S o shall my mûse your name ay coronize,
    I will it blaze to all posterities.

SONETTO. 4. [F. 1 verso]

Relieûe my minde being ouerprest with care,
O heare my sorowes for I doe complaine,
N on may thē help saue you the cure being rare,
A h put me not to death with lingring paine.
L est that my death to you shall nothing gaine,   5
E nforced loûe dislikes which is not meete,
E qualite of loûe doth neuer paine.
Y ou paragon most pretious pure and sweete,
R eioyce your louers harte with loûe for loûe,
V nlace dislike and let be far disdaine,   10
B oth one in one and let affection mooûe :
S ince that in hart affection doth remaine.
V ntie distresse to finde my blisfull sport,
L et not your hart be cruell to the meeke,
A ttend my harts desire in humble sort :   15
S oone grant my humble hart what it doth seeke.

SONETTO. 5. [F. 2 recto]

R etire you thoughts vnto your wonted place,
O r let your place be where your thoughts are prent,
N ewe ioyes approching with a kindely grace :
A nd hope that blossoms on affections dent.
E xcelling worth lyeth buried in my brest,   5
L oue eke concealing paine in tombe of heart,
E ach ioy is griefe wherewith thou art opprest ;
Y ound is thy griefe but sudden old thy smart.
R ich is thy choyce desire hath twise a neede,
E u'n so my hope would reape hope to sustaine,   10
B earing in my heart the wish of heartie deede,
S ealing selfe and lore [sic] high concealed vaine.
V nspotted trust and truth ty'd to the same,
L oue keeping awe is awefull trust shall prooue,
A mongst the stings where heart doth feele the flame,   15
S uch is the meaning of my fixed loue,
    Such be her hart my dolors to remooue.

SONETTO. 6. [F. 2 verso]

Vppon the sandes where raging sea doth roare,
With fearefull sound, I standing with desire,
The element his billowes sendes to shoare,
And takes away my ioy to my great ire.
So water tho did seeke to quench my fire, 5
Whose furie (I beheld) with rash rebound,
That would surflow my life, o rage to dire,
My hearts high rocke was rent which stood on ground :
But high commaund retreait she made him sound,
Who once immite [sic] his furie did surcease, 10
And way-white waûes to vieû her did redound,
Breaking at her sight her empire to complease,
And blustring windes their forces did release,
Least that their tûmult might her eares offend,
And with a calmie fawne breath'd to her ease, 15
Thus was my wish to port they should her send.
    So waûie seas and windes once made me sad,
    So waûie seas and windes haûe made me glad.
        Amore é mare.

SONETTO. 7. [F. 3 recto]

Marching in the plaine field of my conceyte,
I might behold a tent which was at rest,
My forces I did bend but ah deceite :
There left I freedome last which is now least.
For when I thought to fight with Mars for best, 5
There Cupid was which brought me to distresse,
Of foe when I thought to make a conquest,
Loûe and desire in tent did me oppresse.
These captaines twaine from tormēt may surcease,
If they did know the lore I beare in minde, 10
They may as Turtles one procure thy ease,
O that to me of twaine one would be kinde.
    Thou tēt that holdst in night such turtle doûes,
    Reioice, embrace the twayne of world the loûes.

SONETTO. 8. [F. 3 verso]

Of all the bûddes that yeild to men delight,
Sweete eglantine that sentest in the aire,
Art worthie pen of gold thy praise to dight:
Thy flowers of bloome make world both green & faire,
To wearied sence thou comfort doth repaire,   5
Thy pleasure from the eye doth neuer stray,
To fancies hest thou art a stately chaire:
And wounded hartes desire thou canst allay.
More bright then sun thou stand'st in window bay,
And to thy light the sûnne may not come neere,   10
Thou lasting flower doth euerlasting stay:
O that within thy flowers I might appeare.
    As I did passe sweete sent to hart did clime,
    O thou sweete branch the sweetnes of my time.

SONETTO. 9. [F. 4 recto]

As eye bewrayeth the secretes of my minde,
I did regard an Eglantine most faire,
That sprong in sight of sun that brightly shind,
And yet no sunne her springing could empayre.
I did reioyce to come within her aire,   5
Her sweetenes to receiue within my brest:
O that her sent in hart ay might I weare,
With griping griefe heart should not be opprest.
Heart panting sore would cease or take some rest,
And feare disloyall vanish would away,   10
Then ouer griefe in triumph were I blest,
To be reuiued when life went to decay,
    With shadow hide me from these hart-breake showers,
    And with thy sent refresh me in thy bowers.

SONETTO. 10. [F. 4 verso]

The onely helpe that some distressed haûe,
To keepe the life though lingring in the paine,
Is that a time some place will find to saue,
The losse of heart procured by disdaine.
Nowe place is faire yet hope I doe retaine, 5
That distance neuer altereth the minde,
The height of hills doth make the lowly plaine,
The rising sunne in skie feares not the winde:
And yet I see place is somewhat vnkinde,
To offer me the lack of her sweete face, 10
Which cannot solac'd be till I it find:
To free my heart and loûe of loûes disgrace,
  O place if thou didst take her from my eye,
  Bring her in place where place may remedie.

SONETTO. 11. [F. 5 recto]

When chirping byrds did chaunt their musickes layes,
For to salute Dame Flora with her traine,
And vesta cloth'd with chaung of fresh arayes,
For to adorn Hopes happie entertayne:
Then sweetest Briere that shylded our repose, 5
Sent odours sweete, from her fresh hanging bowes,
And Philomel oft-changed notes did close,
Which did accorde eu'n with our hallow'd vowes.
But then; ah then, our discontent began,
A barking Dog step'd foorth with scolding rage, 10
And Musick chang'd to notes of singing Swanne,
That March wee must with swiftest Equipage.
  Loose not sweete bird thy voice, nor brier thy set.
  Wee'le meete againe when fortunes frownes be spent.

F

SONETTO. 12.   [F. 5 verso]

Liue long sweet byrde, that to encrease our ioy,
Made soleme pause, between thy chirping layes,
When stately brier shilded our anoye,
And sheltred vs from peeping Phebus rayes :
Sweet Philomel recorde not our delightes,   5
In Musick's sounde, but to the subtill ayre ;
Least any should participate our spites,
Wrought by a sudden Cerberus repayre.
The pleasing sound our spirites did reuiue,
The sweet, sweet sent, refresh'd our yeilding sence,   10
The happy toutch, most to delight did striue,
But caytiffe dog did hynder our pretence.
  Then happie Byrd farewell, that eas'd my paine,
  Farewell sweet brier, till fortune smile againe.

SONETTO. 13.   [F. 6 recto]

When Lordlin Tytan lodged in the west,
And EBON darknes ou'r-swayde the light,
LATONAS beams decreasing were supprest,
When silent streames did murmur there delight.
Then I entrench'd neere to a noble marke,   5
With courage bould a speare I tooke in hand,
To wyn my will fired with honours sparke,
Or loose my life in my commaunders band.
My speare I broke vpon my gentle foe,
Which being perform'd the second I did charge,   10
But honours force would not be quailed so :
The third I tooke my thoughts for to enlarge ;
  Then call'd I was for treason armes to take,
  And wisedome would my former charge forsake.

SONETTO. 14. [F. 6 verso]

Should feare pale feare me forgoe my minde,
Or legions of monsters make me quaile,
No, no, I was not borne of so base kinde,
As dreadfull sighes would make my heart to faile.
Yet care commaund that honors my conceyte, 5
Made me forsake what my desire embrac'd,
And loth I was that riualls should repeate :
My armes should be by humane force vnlac'd,
Which made me yielde vnto the tyms restraynt,
And leaue the charge of that most noble fight, 10
Where kindnes more then force could make me faint,
To shild my fame from fortunes cancred spite.
  Thus I did charge, thus I discharg'd my launce,
  And so I rest contented with my chaunce.

SONETTO. 15. [F. 7 recto]

As fond conceyt doth moue the wauering minde,
Of artlesse sottes that knowe not wisedoms lore,
Inconstant still to chang with eu'rie winde,
Whose base desires want fruites of vertues store.
So doth the arte and knowledge of the wise, 5
Stirre vp his minde in honors foorde to wade,
With feruent zeale base changlinges to dispise,
And their weake strength, with courage to inuade,
Whose mind being arm'd with true loues strong defence,
He gyrdes his loynes with bondes of constancie, 10
And scornes that ought should alter his pretence,
Or stayne his name, with blot of infamie.
  Thus wisedome is not giuen to manye,
  And but to such for to be constant anye.

Sonetto. 16.

N eu'r-resting chariot of the firie god,
E mbost'd with beames of his eternall light,
W aytes at her beck when she but shakes her rod
O f her commaund; who is the heau'ns delight:
A VRORAS shine doth blush to see her grace,   5
N ymphes gather flowers to make her chaplets fine,
E ngendered griefe my hoped fauour deface,
L oue hates to liue when longing makes it pine:
    E uen so her faire makes longing deere to me,
    H ELEN the faire was not so faire as she.   10

Sonetto. 17.

N o care so great nor thoughts so pining seeme,
E nioying hope to reape the hearts desire:
W hich makes me more your beauties grace esteeme,
O pprest with heate of PAPHOS holy fier.
A ppoint some place to ease my thrauled minde,   5
N ot freed yet from thy late luring looke;
E nioye thy time and solace shalt thou finde,
L et VVLCAN toyle to forge his bayted hooke:
    E yes glorious glaunce will trayne him to the lure,
    H eau'ns do repine thou shouldst his frownes endure.

Sonetto. 18.

N amelesse the flower that workes my discontent,
E ndlesse the cares for her I doe sustaine,
W aste is the soyle which shadowes my content
O nce lende a salue to cure my curelesse paine.
A h deere, how deere I purchase my delight?   5
N ot longe when first I view'd thy sweetest fayre.
E xcept thy beauty lend my darknes light,
L ong shall that looke my heauie lookes ympayre;
    E steeme of him that liues to honour thee,
    H opes true repose shall then be lodg'd in mee.   10

Sonetto. 19. [G. 1 recto]

No sooner I had thy beautie espied,
Cleane washed from the dreggs of vices stayne,
But heart to thee with constant loue was tyed;
And thou perhapps wilt yeilde me but disdayne.
Yf thou wilst not my loue with loue requite, 5
I shall weare out in paine my dismall dayes,
But if thy heart once harbour my delight;
Then shall I liue thy heart to loue and praise.
Yeilde thy consent to cure my fatall wounde,
And let desert preuaile to gayne thy grace, 10
So secret truth shall eu'r in me abounde;
Yf we may meete in some conuenient place;
    And then be sure his name I will deface,
    That should be seene to speake in thy disgrace.

Sonetto. 20. [G. 1 verso]

Campaspe's fayre fresh-paynted forme embrac'd,
By the rare Father of the paynters art,
Could yeilde small ioy except that she had grac'd,
His liuely cunning by her good desart,
Yet he reioyc'd her counterfeyte to kisse. 5
Which she neu'r sawe though he the same profan'd.
How infinite is then my ioyfull blisse,
That still enioy the Idea of thy hande;
Thy gloue it is mine onlye comfort left,
Which thy sweete hande made happie with her touch, 10
This is the Idole that my heart infeoft,
With loues sweete hope which I adore to much.
    That I retayne a monument for thee,
    Though without life; life it affordes to me.

SONETTO. 21. [G. 2 recto]

Sweete ladie I loue, by stelth my loue doth creepe,
Vnto the depth of my profounde conceytes,
Not daring when I wake I dreame a sleepe,
Thus stealing loue by inward signes entreate :
Though merrie gale bydes anchor vp to waye, 5
And canuas store swells with a puffing blaste,
Yet feare of storme doth make vs keepe the baye,
For he is safe that sitts on shoare at laste :
So loue embrac'd when others presence fear'd,
Makes sweete proue sower whē shadowes substance seeme. 10
And Mars himself when Vulcans net he tear'd :
Doth witnes feare doth stolen loue redeeme.
    When sweete repose doth calme the troubled minde,
    Feare of suspect doth leaue his sting behinde.

SONETTO. 22. [G. 2 verso]

My heart enthrаul'd with mine owne desire,
Makes me to be, more then I dare to seeme,
For ielosie may kindle enuies fire,
To hazard that which strength cannot redeeme :
The fayrest rose, on statelyest stalke that growes, 5
Drawes a delight his odours sweete to smell,
Whose pricke sometime doth sting at later close,
Which makes suspect the wished sent t'expell.
Loue prickes my minde to gather fayrest flowers,
And feare forbids lest garden-keeper spie, 10
Whose ielosie raines downe vntimely showres,
And Argos-like doth loues repose discrie.
    Thus doth thy fayre my secret glaunce detect,
    For ielosie doth dayly breede suspect.

SONETTO.   23.   [G. 3 recto]

When sweete repose in loues fayre bower doth rest,
Enchamp'd with vaile of an vnfain'd desire,
Then carefull thoughtes the fearefull mindes inuest,
Lest ARGVS should espie the kindled fire :
For where the dicte of such as may commaunde,   5
Forbidds the same, which louers must embrace,
There feare, and care, together doe demaund ;
Account of thinges which honour may deface :
So is their ioyes with fearefull passions mixt,
Which doth encrease the ardencie of loue,   10
On the forbidden thinges our eyes are fixt ;
Whose accents still doth loues affections moue ;
    Thus stolen loue is eu'r with feare possest,
    For shadowes glymse oft feares the friendly guest.

SONETTO.   24.   [G. 3 verso]

Th'impatient rage of fretting Ielosie,
Suspectes the windes that comes from Cupids winges,
Whose watch preuents the oportunitie,
Whose louers seeke to cure his noysome stinges :
Ech looke, a feare, infuseth to the minde,   5
That gauled is with such a base conceyte,
Which makes them proue to their hearts-ioyes vnkinde.
When loue sweete-ones, of sorrowe, sucke the teate :
Yf one but speake to doe another right,
Suspect sayth then, of smoke there commeth fier,   10
His good deserts are houlden in despite ?
And rancor doth his cruell fate conspire.
    So Ielosie still breedeth base suspect,
    Whose fruitelesse feare there owne good name detect.

SONETTO. 25.

If Argus, with his hundred eyes, did watch
In vaine, when oft loue did his cunning blynde :
Who doubtes but shee that meanes to make a match ?
For to performe both time and place can finde.
And to abridge a woman of her will, 5
Is to powre oyle in fier, to quench the flame :
For then far more she is inclined still,
(Though once despis'd) agayne to seeke the same.
Loue doth commaund, and it must be obayde ;
The sacred deitie of the god is much, 10
Whose maiestie makes louers oft afrayde,
That to his shrine with bended knee they crutch.
  This is the cause, let women beare no blame,
  Who would not play if they did like the game.

SONETTO. 26.

Wheare true desire, (in simpathie of minde)
Hath ioin'd the heartes, with APHRODITES delight,
Mere louing zeale, (to swete aspect inclin'd)
Will finde a time in spite of fortunes might.
ARGVS foresight, whose wake-full heedie eyes 5
Seeke to preuent the wynged Gods commaunde,
Is all to weake his charmes for to surprise ;
Gainst whose resolue his cunning could not stande :
Yet if in Delphos sleepie laye the God,
Authoritie gainst Hundreth eies had fayld, 10
But MERCVRIE, with his enchaunting rod ;
Brought all a sleepe ; when Argus loue assayl'd :
  Then since such happs to watching is assign'd,
  Nothinge is harde where willing is the minde.

SONETTO.   27.   [G. 5 recto]

Daungers altered delayes in loue.

The heart inthraul'd with loues attractiue force,
(Whose hope doth martch with honours equipage,
When reason doth his true desertes remorse)
Must take his time his sorrowes to assuage :
For cheeries ripe will not so long endure, 5
But will in time, fade, wither, and decay,
That which this day, could finest wittes allure ;
To-morrowe, CORIDON doth cast away,
The Iron being hot who list not for to strike,
Shall sure, being colde, neu'r forge it to his minde, 10
And all those partes, moueth loue to like ;
Doe oft (in time) make loue to proue vnkinde.
    Eu'n so in time daunger attends delaye,
    For time and tide for no mans pleasures stayo.

SONETTO.   28.   [G. 5 verso]

Was Io watch'd by Argus in the downes ?
What did not then the winged god inchaunt,
The heardmans eyes, obaying Iunos frownes :
What needes loues crosse so much to make her vaunt,
The brazen tower could not his valour quaile, 5
Who scorn'd that Danae should liue a maide :
Loues inward force gainst enuy will preuaile,
And hap what may : his lawes must be obayd.
What though fayre starre thy glorie is obscur'd :
And cou'rd with a thicke and foggie cloude : 10
Yet Titan when he hath the heau'ns invr'd,
Will cleere the stormes which fatall frownes[1] did shrowde.
    And though that fate abridgeth our delight,
    Yet time I hope will cleare this cloudie spight.

[1] *Printed* frowues.

SONETTO. 29. [G. 6 recto]

The fluent streame, whose stealing course being stayed,
Breakes out vnto a greater deluge rage,
The force of fier with violence delayed,
Makes all thinges weake his furie to asswage :
Desire contrould, will agrauate desire, 5
And fancie crost will fancies force-encrease,
When louing thoughtes will motiue loue inspire,
Enuies oppose can not their bondes release :
Thus currents small doe proue the greatest streames,
Small cinders doe encrease, to raging flame, 10
The hardest hartes are pearc'd with beauties beames,
I hide my griefe yet loue discours the same :
　　　Sweete beautie is the sparke of my desire,
　　　And sparkes in time may breede a flaming fier.

SONETTO. 30. [G. 6 verso]

Sweete beautie in thy face doth still appeere,
Myne onely ioye and best beloued deere :
Myne onlye deere and best belou'd content,
Reuiue my heart and dyinge spirrits spent :
The onlye agent of my thoughtes delight, 5
Embrace my loue and doe not me despight,
Secure my feares and solace cares content,
With hopes repast to fauour mine entent :
The fier will out if fuell doe but want,
And loue in time will die if it be scant : 10
Let then desire yeilde fuell to your minde,
That loue be not blowen out with euerie winde :
　　　So shall my heart like Etnas lasting flame,
　　　Burne with your loue and ioye still in the same.

SONETTO. 31. [G. 7 recto]

I loue, inforst by loues vnlouing charmes,
My loue is pure, my loue is chast, and true,
And that I loue, the greater is my harmes :
Yf loue doth purchase hate, then loue adiew.
Why should not loue be recompens'd with loue,   5
And true desire, obtayne his due desert,
Yf beautie stirre thee to disdayne to moue ?
When mighty stormes oppresse my troubled hart :
Knowe then that truth, may beauties blaze dismay,
And loyall hartes, scorne periur'd beauties pride,   10
Yeilde then in time, prolonge not my delay ?
Lest others should your beauties grace deride :
    So shall your worthes eternished remaine,
    And gaine his loue which others pride disdaine.

To Paris darling. [G. 7 verso]

Were I sheapheard as I am a woodman,
Thy Paris would I be if not thy goodman.
And yet might I performe to thee that dutie,
Yf thou wilt add that fauour to thy beautie.
Nowe that these feastes make other minions frolike,   5
Why is my loue, my doue, so melancholike :
O but I neere gesse, what the cause should be,
Which to tell, tel-tale paper, were but follie ;
Ile therefore for this time conceale it wholye :
For that must counsell betwixt thee and mee,   10
Twixt thee and mee where none may heere nor see.

Buen matina.

Sweete at this mourne I chaunced,
  To peepe into the chamber; loe I glaunced:
And sawe white sheetes, thy whyter skinne disclosing;
And soft-sweete cheeke on pyllowe soft reposing;
  Then sayde were I that pillowe,
Deere for thy loue I would not weare the willowe.

MADDRIGALL. [G. 8 recto]

Madame, that nowe I kisse your white handes later
  Then wild my louing dutie,
  Retayner to thy beautie:
The water crost my wishe, to crosse the water.
Yet thinke not (sweete) those gallants helde thee deerer, 5
Who for thy beauties, then the sunneshine cleerer:
  Eu'n seas vneu'n haue coasted,
  But thou art wise and know'st it:
No; thy **Leander**, whose hartes firie matter,
Cannot be quench'd, by the deuyding water, 10
Will with his oare-like armes quite sheare a sunder
  The waues that floate him vnder:
  Yf when I shall so trie mee,
In thy sweete circled armes I may respire mee.

ROUNDE-DELAY. [G. 8 verso]

Couldst thou none other spite me,
When but once fortune friendly did indite me:
  Thy selfe thou should'st absent mee?
And all vnkinde, vnkinde, to more torment me.
  I haue not thus deserued, 5

To be with tell-tale Tantalus hunger-starued :
    That hauing store of dishes,
I could not feede according to my wishes ?
    But this he for reuealinge,
Gods counsell bide : and I for yours concealing :   10
    In this yet do we varie,
That desert to his, is quite contrary ?
    Then ô most kinde and cruell,
(Except thou minde to starue thy beauties fuell)
    For all my loue, fayth, dutye,   15
Let me but pray, Ipray thee on thy beautie :
    And thou my new-borne dittie,
Desire her for my second dishe but pittie.

MADDRIGALL. [H. 1 recto]

Loue, iust loue, not luste, thus constant liue I :
    My lyfes deere loue mislikes me,
    Yet her sweete fayre doth like me :
Yf loue dislikes ; to like and loue why should I ?
Yf she be coy, why should her loue be trustie ?   5
Yf she be slowe ; why should I be so hastie ?
    Yet loyall hart hath vow'd it,
    And constant truth performes it :
Fayre ; to thy beauties fayre, firme haue I vowed,
Sound is the seede that my resolue hath sowed.   10
But weede is the fruite that my fate hath mowed
    Yet luste I banish, louing
    True zeale, I liue, yet still dying :
Thus still to be constant eu're haue I plowed.[1]

[1] *Printed* plodded.

ROUNDE-DELAY. [H. 1 verso]

Much griefe did still torment me,
In this regard thou doest thy selfe absent me;
   Thy beauty (ah) delightes[1] me?
And this thou know'st to well and therefore spites me.
   So womens mindes doe varie,   5
And change of ayre doth worke quite contrarie;
   Proofe tried my truth and trust too,
Still to be thine, most constant, firme and iust too:
   Therefore shouldest regard me,
And loue for loue (fayre loue) thou should'st award me, 10
   For since I still attend thee,
Howe canst thou choose vnkinde (vnkinde) but friend me,
   Fayne I alone would finde thee,
That my hearts griefe (swete hart) might the vnbinde thee:
   For were I with thee resident,   15
I doubt not I, to be of thy heart president;
   Yeilde then to loue (loue kinde is)
Else would I had byn blinde, eu'n as loue blinde is.

Sinetes Dumpe.   [H. 2 recto]

Ye angrie starrs, doe you enuie my estate.

Immediately following this poem are the verses on Sir John Salusbury's motto, 'Posse & nolle nobile,' by 'Hugh Gryffyth Gent'. (Reprinted by Grosart, in his Introduction, p. xvi; the same lines occur also in the Christ Church MS., fol. 83[b]).

Then comes a separate Title-page:

[1] *Printed* delihgtes.

The
Lamentation of
a Male-content v
pon this Enigma
Maister thy desiers or
liue in Despaire
Ouid
Hoc si crimen eris cri
men amoris eris
Yf this a fault bee
found in me,
Blame loue
that wrought
the misterie.

The Dedicatory Preface runs as follows:

To the Honorable minded
vnknowne, the Name-lesse
wisheth perfect health and
perpetuall happines

Deare Patronesse of my haplesse lamentations; guided by the sterne of thy beauty, which hath the ful commaund of my hart, and wearied with tiranyzing ouer myselfe, in forcible suppressing the agonies of my afflicted minde, by smothering the feruencie of my desires, in the cloudie center of dimme silence: at the last with the raging violence of a stopped streame, for want of course in the intelligible parte of my minde; I am driuen to ouer flowe the bankes of reason, and in despite of my selfe to yeilde vp the raynes to vncontrouled desire; which insuing Poem will fullie manyfest vnto you, with the obseruation of my concealed fancyes: Written vppon a dreame, wherein me thought I heard a voyce from a Cloude pronouncing these wordes ensuing. *Maister thy desires or liue in despaire*, and albeit I helde dreames but phantasies, which commonly doe fall out by contraries; my fortunes being so far inferior to my thoughts, maketh me to doubt the sequell thereof. Yet noble beautie of this sea-bound Region disdayne not to reade ende, and pittie if you will vouchsafe to mitygate the heauines of my martyred heart, which neere stifled with the dampe of my discontentments lamentably beggeth for comfort at your handes.

Yours euer true, secret, and faithfull
Namelesse.

APPENDIX

A COMPLAINT ADDRESSED TO QUEEN ELIZABETH BY SIR JOHN SALUSBURY, KNT., DATED IN THE 44TH YEAR OF HER REIGN

[Star Chamber Proceedings, Public Record Office, Eliz. S$\frac{54}{14}$.]

After reciting in detail the preliminary plots of his adversaries to thwart his election to Parliament as Knight of the shire, which began as soon as the writs for the election were issued, the complainant proceeds :

> The said Sr Richard & his complices yet perceiving the number of the freeholders that had promised their voice with your said subiect [i. e. Sir John Salusbury] to exceed theirs, they the said Sr Richard Trevor, Sr John lloyd, Thomas Price [1] & Thomas Trafford [2] esquiers, all of them then & yet Justices of the peace within your said County together with the said high sherif and John Salusbury Capteine, wherof one being of your Counsell in the Marches of Wales, videlicet Sr Richard Trevor and they togither with Sr John lloyd & the said high sherif, then & yet in the Commission of Oyer & Terminer within the counties of Denbigh, fflint, & Mountgumery, did resolue That since they could not cary the said Eleccion by voyces They would wyn it with blades, and terrefy & daunt any that durst stand in opposicion with them for the same And for that end they not onely themselves assembled & gathered togither by colour of their said auctorityes & especially their said Commission of Oyer & Terminer not out of that County alone but out of diuers other counties neare adioyning seuerall Troopes of wilfull & disordered persones most of them no freeholders, either within your said Countie or elswhere but vagrant & ydle persones meet to committ any villanie whatsoever which they respected not, so as they had armes & weapons & were resolute fellowes, As namely

[1] Sheriff of Co. of Denbigh in 1599; cf. *Hist. MSS. Com.*, Report on Welsh MSS., i. 799.

[2] Thomas Trafford of Treffordd in Esclusham Esq.—See *Archaelog. Cambr.*, Suppl., *Orig. Doc.*, i. p. cccxxxiv, note 2.

Sr Richard Trevor assembled Togither out of the counties of Denbigh, fflint, Salop & Chester, to the number of two hundred persones, or thereaboutes. Sr John lloyd gathered out of the Counties of Denbigh & fflint one hundred persones. Thomas Price to the number of forty persones who marched in seuerall troopes twenty myles through the countie or theraboutes all armed & weaponed with pykes forest bills & other like vnlawfull weapons to the great terror of the Inhabitantes of your said County. Thomas Trafford brought out of his Coale pitte & other places about four score persones. John Salusbury Captein provided against the same tyme out of the Counties of Cayernarvon, Merioneth & Denbigh, to the number of fiftie persones. And the said high sheriff who notwithstanding (by reason of his office) might commaund in any lawful accion the whole power of the said County of Denbigh yet he gathered togither out of the county of Mountgomery & elswhere to the number of one hundred persones or theraboutes. All which persones well furnished with all maner of weapones were appointed to be at Wrexham on the one & twentith day of October last past being the intended day of the said Eleccion. And the said Sr Richard Trevor, Sir John lloyd, Thomas Price, Thomas Trafford togither with the said high sheriffe did not onely themselves vnlawfully assemble togither the persones aforesaid. But did also animate, encourage & perswaide Owin Brereton,[1] Edred Price, esquiers, ffoulke lloyd,[2] John Eaton, Peirce Wynne, Andrew Meredith, Andrew Ellis, Humfrey Ellis, John Wynn . . . John Goulborne, George Puleston, Richard Puleston, John Owin & others whose names are as yet vnknowne (assuring them, That they might lawfully so doe being required by them having aucthority so to doe by vertue of their Commission of Oyer & Terminer. And that your said subiect could not do it without incurring great & eminent danger, by reason that he was not in the said Commission) To procure & labour so many of their freindes as they could to come to the said towne of Wrexham against the said xxjth day of October with such weapons as they could gett. And least they should be vnprouided of Arms & weapons The said Sr Richard Trevor & his said complices caused all the weapons they had to be brought thither against that day. And further the said Sr Richard procured out of the citty of Chester, two wayneloades of Pykes & other weapons to be caryed thither against that day, And fearing least some of them should be destitute notwithstanding the said prouision he called the trayned soldiours of the said hundred of Bromefeild togither and caused them togither with others that came to the muster aforesaid to leave their Armour & weapons behinde them in wrexham which were left in the custody of John Owin of the same towne & others the freindes of the said Sr Richard to furnish such as should be destitute of weapons Which said prouision of men & weapons being so made ready to thende to compell the voices of the ffreeholders by the terror of so many persones armed & weaponed, as

---

[1] Brereton, it is surprising to note, was Sir John Salusbury's brother-in-law; see above, p. xii, note 2.

[2] Sheriff of Co. of Denbigh in 1592; cf. *Hist. MSS. Com.*, Report on Welsh MSS., i. 799.

also to deprive your said subject of his lief, being the greatest obstacle of their hard courses within y^t county. They the said Sr Richard Trevor, Sr John lloyd, Thomas Price Thomas Trafford, John Salusbury Captein with the said high sheriffe who had for his parte likewise laboured diuerse freeholders to be there in like manner came to the said towne of wrexham against the tyme appointed, having their seuerall troopes their readie and the rest of their confederates accordingly, with such Complices & weapons as they could likewise make ready And amongest others the said John Eaton & Peirs Wynn being gentlemen out of the county of fflint, brought thither against the same day fortie persones or theraboutes as namely [the names follow] all armed & weaponed with swordes & daggers longe pyked staves, & such like weapons, and theis & others by the direction of the said Sr Richard Trevor & his Complices, being in the said towne of Wrexham vpon the aforesaid day of the said intended Election, ready to execute & performe such thinges as by him & his said Complices they were required to doe your said subiect with seauen other Justices of the peace of your highnes said county of Denbigh being likewise then & there assembled about the said [four or five words illegible] your Maiesties and seeing many troopes of armed persones flocking vp & downe the streetes there did after one proclamacion then & there made, cause anothir proclamacion to be openly made about eight of the clock of the same day commaunding all persones then & there assembled in your Maiesties name to keep the peace, & laye away their weapons and such as had no voices in the Election to departe presently Which said seuerall proclamacions so made in your Maiesties name The said Sr Richard Trevor with his Complices & adherentes in very vnlawfull troopes assembled brought thither as aforesaid continued still in the presence & view of the aforesaid high sheriffe as he sate at the said county cort without any his Controlement of them or gaynsaying albeyt he was oftentymes desired to dissolue them which argued great partiallity in him the said high sheriffe. By reason wherof the said Sr Richard Trevor having so good oportunity did place in the said church yard of the towne of Wrexham aforesaid, about three hundred persones with pykes gleaves forest Bills welsh hookes longe pyked staves & such like weapons, presuming that your said subiect (being at th'entreatie of his freindes content to forbeare his coming to the place where the County was then kept) would come thither to walke in the Church as all gentlemen at such meetinges usually doe. And your said subiect comming thither accordingly in very peaceable maner accompanied onely with two aged gentlemen & about six other persones, intending to haue gone to walke in the church then & there to haue commouned with his said freindes did as he was in going toward the church meet the said Sr Richard Trevor comming forth of the churchyard accompanied with the said Thomas Trafford John Goulborne Richard Puleston John Wynn Owin, David Trevor, Humfrey Clough, Thomas lloid & diuerse others, to the Number of twenty persones or theraboutes, The said Sr Richard Trevor being armed with a privie Coate & sword & targett, Thomas Trafford with his sworde & sheild, John Goulborne with a sword & targett, Richard Puleston with the like, John Wynn Owin with sworde targett & pistoll,

David Trevor with sword gauntlett & pistoll charged, and all the Rest of the said Company with swordes, targettes, bucklers, pistolls & other like weapons and so armed & arrayed they passed by quietly for y^t tyme & went towardes ye place where ye County cort was kept. And when they were neare thervnto they made a stand & whispered togither and on a sodune retourned hastely towardes ye church againe armed & arrayed as aforesaid where your said subiect being & intending to haue gone into the church with his aforesaid small Company & freindes found the dores thereof fast locked against him with new lockes at & by the appointment & direction of the said Sr Richard Trevor as your said subiect was then & there credibly informed: Whervpon and for that your said subiect did very well knowe that within in the said Church was remayning at the self same tyme all the store of powder of & for ye whole cunty. And neyther knowing & lesse suspecting any parte... [1] malice or plott to be laid for th'endangering of his lief did neuerthelesse resort thither with his said small Company. But fynding the said church dores so locked which ever before were wont at such tymes And occasions... [1] etinge to be kept open And also espying within the said churchyarde the Troope of armed men there placed by the said Sr Richard Trevor as aforesaid And also that the streetes were full of armed persones likewise and doubting what might ensue therof, resolued to giue peaceably back againe vnto his chamber or Lodging with his said small company (consisting of not aboue eight persones besides himself). Howbeit in his said Retourne he mett againe in the Churchyarde the said Sr Richard Trevor... [1] Trafford, John Goulborne, Richard Puleston, John Wynn Owin, David Trevor & the Residue of their Company to the number of twenty or theraboutes as aforesaid All armed & arrayed as afore is shewed Who all at once most desperately drewe and bent their wea[pons] vpon your said Subiect. Whervpon he willed them in your maiesties name to keep your highnes Peace and praying god to preserve your Maiestie aduized them the said Riotters to remember the place they were in and the presente Service then & there to be done for your Ma[iestie] And therwithall according to his Duety reuerently put of his hatt, and still wishing them to keep the Peace said theis wordes God saue the Queene. But before he your said subiect could put on his hatt againe & drawe his sworde to defend himself from them they had persued & driven him vnto the Church wall and their swordes about his eares, to the great hazerd & perill of his lief. Saying & Confirming it with oathes That that should not serve your subiectes tourne. Vpon which said assault there was also a warning peece shott of by former appointment & agreement betweene them the said Sr Richard Trevor & his said partakers of purpose to drawe all their Companies & fforces togither. And vpon the said warning peece so shott of The aforesaid Sr John lloyde knight armed with sword & Buckler, Capteine John Salusbury with sworde & Buckler and a horsemans peece charged, repaired presently thither with their Company, being about two hundred persones, themselves armed & arrayed as aforesaid, And all their said Company with longe pykes long staves, forest Bills gleaves & other like

[1] MS. illegible at this point.

Appendix 85

weapons. And comming so weaponed to the porche or entrie into the said Churchyarde, The said John Salusbury not being able to come nigh your said subiect (at whose lief they aymed) by reason of the great presse of the people asked where the villaine (meaning your said Subiect) was, swearing outragiously, That he would shoote him through. And your said subiect further informeth & sheweth vnto your royal Maiestie, That vpon the shooting of of the warning peece aforesaid There repayred to the aforesaid Riottours & their rude & vnruly Troopes aforesaid, diuerse other wilfull & desperate persones in like riottous & vnlawful manner, As namely the abouesaid Owin Brereton armed with sword & Buckler, George Puleston with the others, George Evans with the like, Henry lloyd of Dacreswoode, with sworde & gauntlett, Randale lloyde with the like, John Kenricke with sworde & dagger, William Jones with sword targett & privy Coate Peirs lloyde with the like, John Owin beinge Constable of your maiesties Peace there having deliuered weapons to many of the freindes of the said Sr Richard who there likewise in his owne persone weaponed with sworde & Buckler not with intent to keep your Maiesties Peace, But to ioyne & take parte with the Riottors aforesaid in their said vnlawfull & wicked Enterprize. So as your said subiect had much adoe to escape aliue out of the handes of the said outragious & rebellious Companies. Neuertheless being by godes good providence deliuered out of their handes, that meant to haue murdred him, and the Tumult being somewhat appeaced, the before named high Sheriffe who had trifled out the tyme all that morning vntill nyne of the Clocke with other petty matters both before & after the said Tumult did not so much as read your Maiesties said writt to him formerly directed as aforesaid. Nor had any purpose to elect your said subiect knight of the shire, Notwithstanding That the greater parte of the ffreeholders then & there assembled were ready to giue their voice with him. But presently dissolued the said county by nyne of the Clock without Electing either knight or Burgesse for your Highnes said Service in your said high Court of Parliament. By reason wherof your Maiesties said Court is defectiue of two members therof, your Highnes said seruice greatly abused, Your said most gratious writt wilfully disobeyed, your said subiect being your Maiesties sworne servaunt (as aforesaid) & your highnes loyall & obedient Subiectes of ye saide County of Denbigh much preiudiced & wronged. And to the full effecting of the said most wicked & vnlawfull outragious & rebellious purpose & plott of the aforenamed Riottors, The aforenamed Thomas Trafford being a Justice of the Peace as aforesaid, did conduct the said Sr Richard Trevor vnto the Churchyard aforesaid there to take view of such armed persones as he had for his parte brought thither, And the said Sr Richard taking viewe of them and being very well pleased therwith yeelded him the said Trafford great thankes for them. All which said armed Companies staying in the towne of Wrexham aforesaid, vntill the said Sr Richard Trevor departed thence which was about foure of the clocke in the afternoone of the aforesaid one & twentith day of October last, attended & guarded him with their weapons aforesaid out of the towne. And at the Townes end he gaue them all harty thankes for their said kyndnes and so rode his way.

In conclusion Sir John Salusbury petitions that writs be directed to Sir Richard Trevor, Sir John Lloyd, and fifty other persons who are mentioned by name, commanding them to appear in person before the Court of Star Chamber to give answer for their conduct at Wrexham as set forth in this complaint.

The manufacturer's authorised representative in the EU for product safety is Oxford University Press España S.A. of El Parque Empresarial San Fernando de Henares, Avenida de Castilla, 2 - 28830 Madrid (www.oup.es/en or product.safety@oup.com). OUP España S.A. also acts as importer into Spain of products made by the manufacturer.
Printed and bound by CPI Group (UK) Ltd, Croydon, CR0 4YY

20/03/2026

02075337-0004